CHARACTERS

MATTY BELL, four fc

DAD, Ben Bell, a far.....

MUM, Mrs Bell

PETE WALCH, a farmer

MRS SCHMIDT, a country school bus driver

TERRY, 'Turbo Tongue', a country schoolboy

KERRY, 'Dingo', a country schoolboy

BUDDAH, a country schoolboy

TEACHER, female country school teacher

LINDSAY ⎫

DAVID ⎭ city school children

BINH, female Vietnamese city school child

MR McKAY, male city school teacher

RADIO,

Spot, an old farm dog

Deek, a farm dog

Snowy, a lamb

A wild dog.

Sheep.

Singers, various

Voices

SETTING

The play is set on a farm in the Australian countryside, at the local area school, at a house in the city and at a city school. The set should use non-naturalistic structures. Costumes should be the same basic kit for all, to which small character details may be added. There should be no additions to perform the animals. Action props should also be non-naturalistic. All sound is made by the actors.

Above: Michael Pope, Barbara Doherty, Chris Tugwell and David Webb shearing the sheep. Below: The Company. Magpie Theatre production. Photos: Jeff Busby.

Contents

Introduction

Chris Johnson

I first met David Holman in 1983. He had been commissioned by Magpie Theatre to write their play for the 1984 Adelaide Festival of Arts. I had been approached to direct it. The writer knew little of the director and the director equally little of the writer. I suspect our first working meeting was saved, for both of us, by the dogs present. The play turned out to be *No Worries* and it remains on the top of the list of my favourite works I've directed.

In November 1988 I arrived in Hong Kong to begin work as Artistic Director of the Chung Ying Theatre Company. I'm the only *gweilo* - foreigner - in a company which rehearses and performs ninety percent of its work in Cantonese. All too soon after starting I needed to select a play and begin to rehearse, in Cantonese, with Chung Ying's actors. I've chosen a play by David Holman. Cantonese or English language aside, I know I can be confident the play will have another language in it we will all be able to understand. Like the three plays presented here, it's a play that depicts a meeting. Characters overcome difference and separation, meet each other and learn something.

The meetings in David Holman's plays are written in the language of theatre, reflecting the language of life - the fragile, often silent language of people meeting and missing, missing and meeting. I'm reminded of the whistle in a pitch that dogs hear but people don't. It's as if David scripts the silent sounds of that whistle for the actors to play out to an audience. Played out, it is a simple, powerful call, responded to and recognised by both children and adults equally. Anyone who has shared in the very full, listening silence of an audience watching the meeting in the sea in *No Worries*, the making and burning of a Mother's Day card in *The Small Poppies*, or a touch during a game in *Beauty and the Beast*, has witnessed the language of David Holman's meetings in action.

In its first season, *No Worries* earned recognition and a respect for theatre for young people, previously unknown in Australia. It shook the certainty of many adults who took it for granted that a play for a child was not a play for them. *The Small Poppies*, directed originally for the 1986 Adelaide Festival by Geoffrey Rush, built on that success. An audience of children and adults came to the theatre to laugh over, cry and celebrate, the memory of their first day at school.

Some people seem surprised that David writes for young people. I think he also writes for dogs - dogs *like* David and they like his plays. Which other writer would describe how he realised that something was out of balance during a rehearsal, by referring to the reaction of his dog? Anyone who has met the dog who owns David will understand. My thanks to David for the three plays published here - and for the one I'm rehearsing at the moment.

Hong Kong, April, 1989

NO WORRIES

No Worries was first performed by Magpie Theatre at Theatre 62, Adelaide, on 6 March, 1984 with the following cast:

MATILDA BELL	Debra Fordham
DAD/KERRY	Chris Tugwell
MUM/BUDDAH	Barbara Doherty
MRS SCHMIDT/	
TEACHER/BINH	Barbara Peirson
MR WALCH/TERRY/	
LINDSAY	Michael Pope
SINGER/DAVID/	
MR McKAY	David Webb

Directed by Chris Johnson
Designed by Ken Wilby
Lighting by Nigel Levings
Musical direction and composition by David Webb

DAVID HOLMAN is an English-born Australian resident with more than seventy plays, films and operas for young audiences to his credit. His work has been produced on every continent and in more than forty countries. Among the most widely produced are *Drink the Mercury* (1973), *No Pasaran* (1977), *The Disappeared* (1980), *Peacemaker* (1981) and *Solomon and the Big Cat* (1988).

No Worries, *The Small Poppies* and *Beauty and the Beast* were all commissioned by the Magpie Theatre and the State Theatre Company of South Australia for three successive Adelaide Festivals. *No Worries* has since been produced in London, Birmingham, Manchester, Chicago, Tel Aviv and Tokyo and *The Small Poppies* in London, Toronto and Tokyo. In 1986 *No Worries* won the Australian Writers' Guild's annual AWGIE Award for Best Children's Drama.

NO WORRIES

THE SMALL POPPIES

BEAUTY AND THE BEAST

by David Holman

CURRENCY PRESS • SYDNEY

CURRENCY PLAYS
General Editor: Katharine Brisbane

First published in 1989 by
Currency Press Pty. Ltd.,
P.O. Box 452 Paddington, N.S.W. 2021.
Australia.

National Library of Australia
Cataloguing-in-Publication data
Holman, David, 1942-
No worries ; The small poppies ; Beauty and the beast

   ISBN 0 86819 181 7
   1. Title. II. Title: No worries. III. Title: The small
   poppies. IV. Title: Beauty and the beast.

A822'.3
Typeset by Allette Systems Pty. Ltd. Sydney
Printed by Australian Print Group, Maryborough

Currency's creative writing program assisted by the
Australia Council, the Federal Government's
arts funding and advisory body.

ACT ONE

The cast mingle with the young audience as they arrive and introduce themselves and chat. When the audience is in, one of the band plays a chord and the band goes into 'Waltzing Matilda' (Queensland version). They then go immediately into 'Road to Gundagai'. As soon as the song is over all the singers shout:

ALL: [*to the audience*] G'day.
[*They get the audience to respond, then play a folk ballad musical intro.*]

SINGER: Today we're going to do a story for you called *No Worries*. Or *The Ballad of Matilda Bell*. It goes something like this:

SINGERS: Come gather round you children,
             A story I will tell
             About a bold young bushie girl;
             Her name's 'Matilda Bell'.

[*Over the following,* MATTY *indicates herself at appropriate moments.*]
             She'll trap a rabbit, catch a yabbie
             In the twinkle of an eye,
             Though she won't be ten until next year
             And she's only four feet high.

SINGER: [*singing badly*]
             Waltzing Matilda, waltzing Matilda,
             You'll come a-

SINGERS: [*interrupting*]
             Now there's just six of us to tell
             The tale of 'Tilda Bell
             And we'll be playing people
             But cars and sheep as well ...

WALCH: ⎱ [*together*]   Brmmm-mmm-mmm ...
DAD: ⎰   Baaa-aaa-aaa ...

SINGERS: So don't get agitated
             If he comes on as a clock ...

WALCH: Tick tock, tick tock ...

SINGERS: Then turns around and comes back on
As a shearer or a chook.

SINGER: [*singing badly*]
'Click' go the shears, boys,
'Click, click, click' -

SINGER: [*interrupting, to the audience*] I don't reckon you're
going to get agitated about that, are you? Him coming on
as an alarm clock, or a chook and lots of different people
in Matilda's story?
[*The audience responds.*]
No? No worries.

SINGERS: Now life ain't all roses,
As some of you will know,
And something's coming up real soon'll
Bring poor Matty low.

They say that big girls, they don't cry,
But you know that ain't true,
'N' tears are goin' come to Matty's eyes
'D turn an ocean blue.

SINGER: Big girls do cry,
Big girls do cry -

SINGERS: [*interrupting*]
But all that's in the future,
So if it's alright with you
We'll get Matilda's tale a-goin'
Without much more ado ...

[MATTY, *her* DAD *and* PETER WALCH *sit in position for the
scene in the utility to follow. The wild dog sits at a distance.
The lights go down on all except the remaining two singers
who sit apart from the others. The music slows.*]
It's midnight in the paddock,
Sheep sleeping in the dust.
A hungry killer creeping up
With eyes as red as rust.

[*A spot finds the head of the wild dog. Pause. It turns its
head, licks its lips and sniffs. Then there is a distant sound.
It listens.*]

WALCH: [*softly, growing louder*] Brmmm-mmm-mmm ...

[*The dog listens.*]

SINGER: And here comes Matilda!

[*A roving spot snaps on, but it doesn't find the dog.* WALCH's *car noise gets louder. Lights go up on the three in the ute:* MATTY *on the spotlight, her* DAD *with the gun and* WALCH *driving. When* WALCH *isn't speaking he makes car noises.*]

WALCH: Brmmm-mmm-mmm. See anything, Matilda?

MATTY: Not yet, Mr Walch.

DAD: Careful over this rise, Pete. My sheep are too weak to move fast.

WALCH: Well, if they can't hear this old engine, they're deaf as well as hungry.

DAD: We've lost her I reckon.

[*The dog's head moves. It listens and licks its lips.*]

MATTY: We'll get her, Dad.

DAD: No, I reckon we've lost her.

MATTY: Aw, Dad!

DAD: And you've got school tomorrow morning, young lady. Pete!

MATTY: Aw, school, Dad? There's no worries there.

DAD: Your new teacher told your mother there is worries. Told her at the footy, Saturday.

MATTY: When?

WALCH: Back to the house, Ben?

DAD: I reckon.

WALCH: Brmmm-mmm-mmm ...

DAD: Yes. Told your mother if you spent as much time with your books as you do on that basketball team of yours, she'd be a very happy woman.

MATTY: Aw, Dad.

[WALCH *screeches to a halt.*]

DAD: What's the matter, Pete?

[WALCH *mimes opening the ute door.* WALCH *or one of the singers make a very accurate opening and closing sound.* WALCH *walks a little way and concentrates on something on the ground.*]

What is it, Pete?

WALCH: [*waving*] Matilda!

[MATTY *swings the light across.* WALCH *bends down.*]

Two of yours, Ben.   Throats ripped out.   Blood still
dripping.
[*He looks at the direction of the marks.*]
This way.
[WALCH *runs back to the ute.*]

DAD: Bludging ...
[WALCH *opens the door and gets in to the same sound
effects, though quicker. He switches the engine on and
pulls the ute into a swift turn.* MATTY *and* DAD *sway.
Music.*]
Fox, do you think?

WALCH: Might be. Brmmm-mmm-mmm ...
[*They drive.*]

MATTY: There Dad!

DAD: Where?
[MATTY *swings the light and it glances off the dog.* WALCH
manoeuvres the ute.]

WALCH: Brmmm-mmm-mmm. Yes. Brmmm-mmm-mmm ...
[*The car swings around and chases the dog to guitar
accompaniment. Frightened, the dog looks this way and
that. The ute swings about.*]
You alright, Matilda?

MATTY: [*swinging the light*] No worries, Mr Walch.

DAD: Keep that light steady, I've lost her.
[*The dog is hit by the full glare of the light.*]

MATTY: There, Dad!

DAD: Ah, good.
[*He lines up the sights.*]
Pete, keep it steady. Good. Now ...
[*Pause.* DAD *makes the sound of a shot. The dog's face
twitches, grimaces, and his tongue lolls out. The dog falls.
It's not quite dead.* WALCH *slams the car to a halt.*]

WALCH: D'you hit her?

DAD: Yeah.

MATTY: [*jumping down*] Can I go see, Dad?

DAD: Be careful!
[MATTY *takes the gun, goes to the dog and looks.*]

MATTY: Looks like a city dog, Dad. It's got a collar on.

DAD: I'd like to get my hands on the slicker who dumped that.
Is she dead?

[MATTY *kills it with a blow to the head.*]

MATTY: It is now.

[DAD *and* WALCH *come to look as she turns the dog over to check it is dead.* WALCH *pats her on the head. She smiles.*]

DAD: [*turning to the ute*] Now, bedtime for you, young lady.

MATTY: Aw, Dad. Maybe there might be another one.

DAD: I said bed.

WALCH: You've done a good job, Matilda.

MATTY: Aw, thanks, Mr Walch.

DAD: Yes. And she'd be out here all night if I let her and that'd get me into trouble with her mother.

WALCH: Yeah.

DAD: So bed.

MATTY: Awright, Dad. Can I drive home?

DAD: Awright. Come on.

[*They get into the ute.* MATTY *climbs on her dad's knee and takes the wheel. As she drives, music and lights slowly fade on her delighted face.* DAD *and* WALCH *exit. The* RADIO *takes up its position.*]

[*Off*] Are you in bed, Matilda?

[*The lights fade up to reveal* MATTY *next to her bed. The* RADIO *is next to her.*]

MATTY: A minute, Dad.

DAD: [*off*] I'm turning off the light in two minutes. And don't forget your prayers.

MATTY: Awright Dad.

[*She adopts an attitude of prayer.*]

[*Quickly*] As I lay me down to sleep I pray the Lord my soul to keep. [*More slowly*] Jesus, thanks for telling Uncle Kev about the radio alarm I wanted. It came this arvo. He says it's the same make as the one he's got in his cab in the city. Listen, it's far out. You can get Eight KLR.

[*She hits the top of the* RADIO*'s head, or turns its nose.*]

RADIO: - Cigarette that bears a lipstick's traces, an airline ticket -

MATTY: [*punching its head*] Urghhh. You can -

MATTY: ⎫ [*together*] - Get Eight Triple R ...
RADIO: ⎭ - Water trains to areas where the farmers
are applying for drought status. In a tough statement, the
Premier -
MATTY: [*punching down*] You can get Eight ZW.
RADIO: - Century by Alan Border at Lords today. It was the
quickest century so far of the English summer, and ...
DAD: [*off*] Matilda!
[MATTY *punches down for the last time and dives into bed.*]
MATTY: It's alright, Dad. I'm in bed. [*Sotto voce, to Jesus*]
Yeah, and you can get four city stations. It's unreal. Jesus,
can you do anything for us about some rain? Dad's real
down about it and the lambs are awful thin and crook ...
Well, you're a lamb yourself, so I reckon they've told you
that already. A few points, Jesus, or they won't last the
month.
DAD: [*off*] Now, Matilda!
MATTY: Half a minute, Dad. [*Quickly, whispering*] Jesus,
we're playing Katunga on Saturday and Mum and Dad are
coming to the game, so -
DAD: [*off, interrupting*] Turning the light off, Matilda!
MATTY: G'night, Dad.
DAD: [*off*] G'night. See you tomorrow.
[*The lights go out. Darkness. Pause.*]
MATTY: [*whispering*] Sorry, Jesus. If we beat Katunga we can
still catch Taterloo before the end of the season.
DAD: [*off*] Matilda!
MATTY: [*almost inaudibly*] Thanks, Jesus. G'night.
SINGERS: [*softly*]
        Waltzing Matilda, waltzing Matilda,
        You'll come a-waltzing, Matilda, with me ...

RADIO: Tick tock, tick tock, tick tock ...
MATTY: Yeah, we'll beat 'em.
    [*She gives a small snore.*]
SINGERS: Matilda dreams through one o'clock
           And two and three and four,
           Dreaming of the big game
           And the baskets she will score.

Then at six her dad goes out
To find the rain gauge dry as dry
And he looks up and he swears aloud
At another empty sky.

[MATTY *snores. The lights fade up.*]

RADIO: Tick, tock, tick tock, brrr-rrr-rrr.

[*The* RADIO *sings a jingle.*]

MATTY: Ahhh.

[*She reaches out, but the radio moves away. Without getting up,* MATTY *tries to get at the* RADIO *to turn it off without success.*]

RADIO: This is Eight Triple R in Katunga. Last night was dry nationwide, apart from a small fall in Western Australia. Today's top temperature is predicted a cool ten degrees, so if you're a man on the land, why not drop into Big Ron Veiver's big sale; that's Ron's Second-Hand Farm Equipment Centre in Katunga for the best used tractors, headers and tillers, open at eight -

[MATTY *finally succeeds and the radio falls silent.*]

MUM: [*off*] Matilda, are you up?

[*She isn't.*]

MATTY: Yes, Mum.

MUM: [*off*] Breakfast in ten minutes. I don't want you late for the bus again. Are you washed?

MATTY: [*getting up*] Just doing it, Mum.

[*She shakes her head and mimes a basketball throw.*]

Katunga, zero. Yorktown Junior All Stars, one hundred and forty-nine.

MUM: [*off*] Matilda!

[MATTY *goes a couple of steps to the mirror. An actor plays her reflection, doing the precise mirror image of all* MATTY's *movements.* MATTY *wipes the mirror, then looks into it. She makes a face and turns on the tap. Someone makes the right noise.* MATTY *turns off the tap, washes her hands and dabs her face.*]

[*Off*] Properly!

[MATTY *gives her face a little bit more of a wash. She pauses, satisfied.*]

[*Off*] Don't forget your neck!

MATTY: [*yelling*] Mum, this bore water's browner than yesterday. I'm just making myself dirty.

MUM: [*off*] No excuses.

[MATTY *does her neck and then reaches for an imaginary towel. She finds it, wipes her face and throws it on the floor.*]

[*Off*] Matilda, you haven't thrown the towel on the floor again, have you?

[*The reflection looks at* MATTY *and shakes its head smugly.* MATTY *looks daggers at the mirror.*]

MATTY: No, Mum.

[MATTY *and the reflection pick up their towels. As they smooth the towels on their rails the reflection looks smug, then returns to a mirror of* MATTY's *actions.* MATTY *picks up toothpaste and brush and does her teeth while looking at her reflection. She finishes and replaces them in the rack.*]

MUM: [*off*] Breakfast on the table.

MATTY: Coming, Mum.

[MATTY *turns to go, then realises she hasn't taken the plug out. She does so and watches the water disappear to the appropriate sound effect.* MATTY *and her reflection look at each other and shake hands. Both exit.* MUM *enters with an imaginary bowl of cereal. As* MATTY *enters* MUM *gives it to her. As she eats, someone does the effects of the spoon in the bowl and eating noises.*]

MUM: Didn't your new teacher give you any homework this week, Matilda?

[MATTY *shakes her head and eats.*]

Are you sure?

[MATTY *nods and eats.*]

No?

[MATTY *finishes.*]

MATTY: No. [*Handing back the bowl*] Thanks, Mum. I'm just going to feed Snowy.

MUM: [*taking the bowl out*] Feed the chooks first.

MATTY: Awright, Mum.

[MUM *exits. The singers move their heads in chook-like fashion and make appropriate noises.*]

Awright, I'm coming.

[MATTY *reaches for imaginary feed and starts to cast it. The chooks go for it.*]

[*Spreading feed*] Snowy! Snowy!

[*Snowy the lamb enters and pushes up to her.* MATTY *picks up an imaginary feeding bottle. Snowy gets stuck into it.* MATTY *strokes the lamb.*]

Awright, Snowy, how many sides has an octagon? And what's a rhomboid? The stupid questions this teacher asks you. You don't know?

[*Spot, the old farm dog, enters and circles Snowy.*]

It's alright, Spot. Your working days are over. You leave it to the young ones. Go on, go and lie on your rug. Good dog.

[*She pats him and Spot goes, rather put out.*]

Awright, Snowy, that's enough. I've got to catch the school bus. G'bye, Mum.

[MUM *appears with an imaginary bag and gives it to* MATTY.]

MUM: There's your lunch. G'bye, Matilda.

MATTY: G'bye, Dad!

[DAD *appears.*]

DAD: G'bye, Matilda. You're late.

MATTY: Not really, Dad. G'bye.

[MATTY *goes. Snowy remains.* DAD *looks at the sky in all directions. Nothing. He is fed up.*]

MUM: They had rain in W.A.

DAD: Yeah.

MUM: What are you thinking about, Ben?

DAD: Noah. You know, that lucky so and so in the Bible.

MUM: We've got nothing in the freezer, Ben, for tea.

[DAD *nods. Pause. He takes hold of Snowy.*]

Aw, not that one, Ben. That's Matilda's.

DAD: It's not Matilda's and she's getting too attached to it.

MUM: Aw, Ben.

DAD: She always gets too attached to them. I've told her.

MUM: Ben!

DAD: [*to Snowy*] Come on.

[DAD *exits with Snowy. Music.* MUM *looks at the sky. Pause. She goes.*]

SINGERS: Matty runs on through the morning,
            Runs on through the land.

[MATTY *enters and runs on the spot.*]
            Where once the grass came to her knee
            Now there's just drifting sand.

            And lambs bleat silently
            As past them Matty flies,
            And crows above in circles
            Swoop down to peck their eyes.

[*The singers bleat silently over the music break while* MATTY *pants as she runs. Distantly comes the sound of the school bus.*]
            Run, Matty, run; it's eight, you're late.
            The road's a cloud of dust.
            Inside of it is Mrs Schmidt
            Who drives the old school bus.

[MRS SCHMIDT *and the two boys* KERRY *and* TERRY *take their position on the bus.* SCHMIDT *does the bus noises as the song continues.* MATTY *waves her arms.*]
            Drives that bus like Allan Jones
            In the Australian Grand Prix,
            'N' told the kids a million times
            She don't wait for nobody!

MATTY: [*breathlessly*] Mrs Schmidt! I'm here.

[SCHMIDT *does the effects as the bus brakes: a big sound. The kids roll forward and yell in protest.* SCHMIDT *does the sound of the door opening.*]

KERRY: ⎫
TERRY: ⎭ [*together*] G'day, Matilda.

SCHMIDT: G'day, Matilda. It's lucky for you I'm a couple of minutes late. I've -

KERRY: ⎫
TERRY: ⎬ [*together*] - Told you kids a million
SCHMIDT: ⎭ times: I don't wait for nobody.

[SCHMIDT *makes the sound of the doors closing and starts off.*]

SCHMIDT: Brmmm-mmm-mmm.

MATTY: [*heading back*] Thanks, Mrs Schmidt.

SCHMIDT: Where d'you think you're going, Matilda?

KERRY: Here, Matilda!

MATTY: Up the back seat, Mrs Schmidt.

SCHMIDT: Aw, no. Not after yesterday. My bus isn't a
basketball court. You sit there.

MATTY: Awww!

SCHMIDT: And remember ...

ALL: I've got eyes in the back of my head.

[*The kids make faces as the bus speeds on.*]

TERRY: D'you see Benny Hill last night?

KERRY: [*ignoring* TERRY] Eight KLR says there's going to be
rain.

MATTY: Yeah?

SCHMIDT: That's the fourth time this year Eight KLR have
said that and they haven't been right yet.

KERRY: Yes, but they had twenty points in W.A. last night.

SCHMIDT: [*pointing out the window*] It had better for O'Hara's.
Look at them.

[*All the children look out of the window to see the
drought-ravaged sheep.*]

MATTY: He overstocks.

KERRY: Yeah. Always did, my dad says.

TERRY: I did.

KERRY: Did what?

TERRY: See Benny Hill last night. Watch. He did this.

[TERRY *does his Benny Hill impression, which nobody takes
any notice of.*]

KERRY: My dad said you got the wild dog last night.

MATTY: Aw yeah. No worries.

SCHMIDT: What dog was that, Matilda?

MATTY: A city dog, Mrs Schmidt. It's been killing over at
our place.

KERRY: And ours.

TERRY: You're not watching! I'm doing this for you.

SCHMIDT: I saw a dog parked down this road a couple of months
back. A puppy.

MATTY: What colour?

SCHMIDT: Kind of brown.

MATTY: This one was black.

SCHMIDT: The blokes who did it won't do it again, I reckon.

KERRY: Why? What did you do?

SCHMIDT: Well, I was in the old truck going past when I saw them throw this puppy out ...

KERRY:
MATTY: } [*together, interested*] Yeah?

TERRY: Did anyone see *Dallas*?

MATTY: Turbo Tongue! [*To* SCHMIDT] Yeah?

SCHMIDT: A couple of city slickers from interstate. New South.

KERRY: What, the car was stopped, was it?

SCHMIDT: Yeah, so I pulled in in front of them and then I just backed the old truck right into them.   It was a new Commodore.

KERRY:
MATTY: } [*together*] Far out! Aw yeah.

SCHMIDT: Did a little panel beating for them.

KERRY: Yeah.

SCHMIDT: [*watching the road*] Nicole Farmer's not at the stop. Now I've told -

MATTY: [*interrupting*] Aw, she had a toothache yesterday arvo...

KERRY: Her mum'll be taking her into that dentist in Katunga.
      [SCHMIDT *speeds up again.*]

SCHMIDT: Brmmm-mmm-mmm.

MATTY: His breath, that dentist.

KERRY: Yeah, like an emu's armpit.

SCHMIDT: Kerry!

TERRY: Sue Ellen had to go to the dentist in last night's -

KERRY: [*interrupting, moving to* MATTY] Matilda, have you done the homework? What's a rhomboid?

MATTY: I don't know.

KERRY: Let's have a look at your book.

TERRY: Yeah, she'd been drinking again and Cliff Barnes ... Hey, I'm talking to you. Hey!
      [*The singers play a musical intro to the ballad.*]

SINGERS: The bus rolls on through country roads,
              The dust is flying high,
              'N' failing crops and signs for clearing
              Sales what meets the eye.

In the back seat playing two-up
For lollies, country rules.
Then at half-past eight they reach the gate
Of the Yorktown Area School.

[*Noise comes from the bus as the kids pile towards the door.*]

SCHMIDT: Have a good day! See you this arvo!

[*As the kids get off the bus,* BUDDAH *enters with an imaginary basketball.*]

BUDDAH: Matilda!

MATTY: [*turning*] Yeah?

BUDDAH: Catch!

[BUDDAH *throws the ball.* MATTY *catches. The others respond.*]

KERRY: Matilda, I'm on your side.

TERRY: Aw, no!

BUDDAH: [*indicating the other side*] Turbo Tongue. [*To* MATTY] D'you catch that fox last night?

MATTY: It wasn't a fox. It was a wild dog.

BUDDAH: D'you shoot it?

MATTY: Aw yeah. No worries. We're Australia.

KERRY: Aw yeah!

TERRY: What are we?

KERRY: You can be New Zealand.

BUDDAH: Aw no. Why do we always have to be New Zealand? They're morons.

TERRY: We'll be the Yanks. They're all about two metres tall.

BUDDAH: Two metres fifteen, some of them.

TERRY: Yeah, Yanks!

KERRY: Look, you can be who you like, you're not going to beat Australia.

TERRY: Hurry up, the bell'll be going.

MATTY: Awright, it's one minute to go in the second half. Olympic final.

TERRY: Aw, yeah.

MATTY: It's Australia a hundred points, U.S.A. a hundred.

TERRY: Aw, no, that's not fair.

BUDDAH: We want odds. Two points difference. You've got ninety-eight.

MATTY: Awright. Minute to go. We've got to get two baskets. Ready?

[*She bounces the imaginary ball, doing the appropriate sound effects. Over the following she bounces the ball cleverly from one side to the other.*]

SINGER: Waltzing Matilda, waltzing Matilda,
                 You'll come a-

SINGERS: [*interrupting*]
                 So now you all will see how
                 Waltzing 'Tilda got her name:
                 Best backboard queen you've ever seen
                 And basketball's her game.

                 And in her mind she isn't four feet high,
                 She's one metre ninety-three,
                 And there ain't no way the U.S.A.'s
                 Going to beat the Wallabies.

[MATTY *darts forward.* BUDDAH *and* TERRY *guard with hands up.* KERRY *positions to take a pass.*]

KERRY: Matilda!

[MATTY *fakes a pass to* KERRY. TERRY *buys it.* MATTY *goes past and shoots. They watch above them. The ball bounces on the rim and goes in.* MATTY *and* KERRY *leap.*]

TERRY: Aw, no!

KERRY: ⎫
MATTY: ⎭ [*together*] Australia!

KERRY: A hundred each.

SINGER: [*into an imaginary mike*] This is Ian Chappell for Channel Nine at the Olympic Final. The scene here is really fantastic. The Wallabies led by Matilda Bell, this pint-sized prodigy from the bush, have levelled the score against the U.S.A. with twenty-seven seconds on the clock. Back to the action.

[BUDDAH *takes the ball.* KERRY *and* MATTY *guard, hands up.* TERRY *gets into position.* BUDDAH *passes.* KERRY *intercepts.*]

TERRY: Aw, no, Buddah, you ding dong!

MATTY: Dingo!

[BUDDAH *attempts to cut off the pass.* KERRY *looks up.*]

KERRY: Matilda!

[*He throws to* MATTY.]

TERRY: [*to* BUDDAH] Dev!

SINGER: [*still as Ian Chappell*] Seventeen seconds on the clock.

KERRY: To me!

TERRY: Buddah!

BUDDAH: I'm marking.

SINGER: [*still as Ian Chappell*] Thirteen.

KERRY: Shoot, Matilda!

MATTY: Can't.

[*The action freezes.*]

SINGER: [*still as Ian Chappell*] This is fantastic. With ten seconds on the clock, Matilda has the ball. This will be the last chance of the game. Seven seconds. She's too far out, surely. Five. But she shoots ...

[MATTY *shoots. They watch as it loops towards the net. It hits the rim and circles.* BUDDAH, *under the basket, watches it go round and round.*]

It's rolling round the rim. Three seconds. It'll be a drawn game if ... Two. Still rolling. One. And it drops.

[*The sound of ringing comes from off. A* TEACHER *appears with the bell.*]

TEACHER: [*off*] Into school, children.

MATTY: ⎫
KERRY: ⎭ Australia!

[*They start to move in.*]

MATTY: Buddah, you're going to need to defend better than that if we're going to beat Katunga Saturday. [*To all*] Full practice tomorrow, awright?

[*The others nod.*]

TEACHER: [*off*] Into school, children!

[*The bell continues. Over the following the kids make lots of noise as they climb into their imaginary desks. The class includes* BUDDAH, KERRY, TERRY *and* MATTY.]

SINGERS: So in they go, there's Red and Ted,
Into the Area School.
There's Bill the Bear and Einstein
And Turbo Tongue O'Toole,

> There's Dingo Dale and Buddah
> And Waltzing Matilda Bell:
> The noise they make's a small earthquake;
> It's Year Five, ain't they swell.

[*The* TEACHER *stands out front at the imaginary board.*]

TEACHER: Thank you. Good morning.

KIDS: G'morning, Miss.

TEACHER: Now, Matilda, come out and draw me an octagon.

MATTY: [*to* KERRY, *whispering*] Octagon?

[MATTY *gets up.*]

Miss, I know what a rhomboid is.

TEACHER: No. An octagon. Come on. This was your homework.

[*She holds out the imaginary chalk and* MATTY *takes it. The* TEACHER *turns away.* MATTY *looks lost. Out of sight of the* TEACHER, *she looks around and* KERRY *holds up eight fingers.* MATTY *turns back to the board as the* TEACHER *turns back.*]

MATTY: One, two, three, four, five, six, seven, eight.

TEACHER: Good. Well done, Matilda. [*To* TERRY] Em ...

TERRY: I'm Terry, Miss. Miss, I saw your boyfriend yesterday arvo.

TEACHER: 'Afternoon'.

TERRY: Yes Miss.

TEACHER: No you didn't, Terry.

TERRY: I did, Miss.

TEACHER: Well, you must have extremely powerful eyes then, Terry. My boyfriend is six hundred and fifty kilometres south of here in the city. Now. A septagon.

[TERRY *comes forward. The chalk is held out.*]

MATTY: Aren't you ever going to see him again, Miss?

KERRY: Do you miss him, Miss?

TEACHER: [*to* TERRY] Septagon.

[TERRY *looks around for help and* KERRY *holds up ten fingers.* TERRY *starts to draw.*]

BUDDAH: What's his name, Miss?

TEACHER: Yes I do miss him and his name's 'Bruce'. Now that's enough. No, Terry, a septagon has seven sides.

OTHERS: [*whispering to each other*] Bruce.

TEACHER: Now. Alright. [*Taking out imaginary papers*] You did some writing for me yesterday on the subject 'A day to remember'. Yes, Kerry, very good. Last year's basketball championship, you made that sound very interesting.

KERRY: Yeah, Miss. We totalled Timeroo.

TERRY: Matilda got twenty-two points.

TEACHER: Terry, is this your paper?

TERRY: Yes, Miss.

TEACHER: It's only got your name on it.

TERRY: I couldn't think of anything, Miss.

TEACHER: Matilda, you wrote a lot, good, but I can't read it. What does that say?

MATTY: 'Mouse', Miss.

TEACHER: 'M', 'O', 'W', 'S'?

MATTY: Yes, Miss.

TEACHER: 'M', 'O', 'U', 'S', 'E'. Read it to us.

MATTY: Aw, Miss.

TEACHER: Come on. I'm sure it's very good.

MATTY: 'The day the mouse plague came to Yorktown.'

OTHERS: Aw yeah!

MATTY: 'The harvest was good three years ago and then the mouses came.'

TEACHER: 'Mice'.

MATTY: Mice. 'First time they came was at night. My dad and me -'

TEACHER: [*interrupting*] 'I'.

MATTY: I ... 'was -'

TEACHER: [*interrupting*] 'Were'. You and your dad. Plural.

MATTY: Were 'in the ute coming back from the dam. I was driving on his knee. The ute started slipping on the road. Dad took the wheel. I thought it must be oil or something. But then we saw the road moving.'

TEACHER: What?

KERRY: Aw yeah, Miss, it looks like that.

TERRY: Haven't you ever seen one, Miss?

KERRY: Aw, when they came to our place -

TEACHER: [*interrupting*] Alright. Later. Matilda.

MATTY: 'It was mouses ...' mice ... 'millions of them.'

TEACHER: 'Millions'?

KIDS: Aw yeah.

TERRY: They were in here, Miss. In the teacher's desk.

TEACHER: What?

KERRY: Aw yeah, Miss Eaton ... they were all in her hair once ... right where you are now, Miss.

BUDDAH: She had to go back to the city for a month to rest.

TEACHER: Go on, Matilda.

MATTY: 'Next day we got an air compressor -'

KERRY: ⎫
TERRY: ⎬ [*together*] Aw yeah.

KERRY: We made this trap, Miss. A bit of cheese and a ladder. Caught plenty in a tin.

MATTY: Kerry held the mouse and put the tube down its throat.

KERRY: Aw yeah.

MATTY: And then we turned on the air.

TERRY: Booom.

KERRY: Spluuurg.

MATTY: That's as far as I got, Miss.

TEACHER: [*horrified*] Down it's throat?

KERRY: Aw yeah, the shed wall was covered with their guts.

MATTY: And brains.

TEACHER: [*moving off*] Will you read your *Treasure Island*s for a few minutes, please?

TERRY: What's the matter, Miss?

[*The* TEACHER *puts her hand over her mouth.*]

TEACHER: Headache.

[*The* TEACHER *exits. The kids look bemusedly after her.*]

MATTY: Bruce.

KERRY: [*to* TERRY] Bruce, darling.

[*He goes to kiss him as the bell rings.*]

TEACHER: Recess!

[*Music. All noisily get up.* MATTY *moves away from the other three and each side draws an imaginary chalk line.*]

BUDDAH: ⎫
KERRY: ⎬ [*together*]
TERRY: ⎭

> Charlie over the water,
> Charlie over the sea.
> Charlie broke a teapot
> And blamed it onto me.

MATTY: Kerry.

[*The three move forward with alacrity.* MATTY *catches*
KERRY. *They go back to* MATTY'*s line while the others
return to the opposing line.*]

BUDDAH: ⎫ [*together*]
TERRY: ⎭

Charlie over the water,
Charlie over the sea.
Charlie broke a teapot
And blamed it onto me.

MATTY: ⎫ [*together*] Buddah.
KERRY: ⎭

[BUDDAH *and* TERRY *move forward.* MATTY *and* KERRY
tag BUDDAH. TERRY *starts to get excited as they return to
their lines.*]

ALL: Charlie over the water,
Charlie over the sea.
Charlie broke a teapot
And blamed it onto me.

MATTY: ⎫
KERRY: ⎬ [*together*] Turbo Tongue.
BUDDAH: ⎭

[TERRY *moves forward, then stops and points behind them.*]
TERRY: Hey look! Behind you! Clouds. It's going to rain.
KERRY: Not that old trick.
TERRY: I swear on the Bible. Look. Rain!
[*They look around.* TERRY *gives a yelp and runs through
them, laughing, without being caught. They move towards
him.*]
It was only a joke. No!
KERRY: Get him!
[*They scrag* TERRY. *Everyone piles on top of him. A dog
enters and barks at them, trying to break up the fight.*]
MATTY: It's alright, boy. It's only a game.
[BUDDAH *takes out his imaginary lunch.*]
TERRY: Whose dog is he?
MATTY: The new bloke down at the bank. He doesn't look
after him. I'm training him.
KERRY: Aw yeah.
MATTY: You watch.
BUDDAH: What's his name?

MATTY: 'Deek'. 'De Castella', aren't you, boy? Give me a bit of your sanger. I'll show you. Deek. I taught him this. Deek. Stay. He'll do it. Stay.

[*She moves away with the bit of sandwich. After a short pause, Deek follows.*]

KERRY: Aw yeah. Barbara Woodhouse.

MATTY: He'll do it. Deek. Sit. If you want the sanger you sit. Deek. Sit.

BUDDAH: I've seen better trained camels.

MATTY: Deek. Sit. Sit. He usually does it. He just don't feel like it at the moment. Deek. Sit.

TERRY: The dog can't do anything.

MATTY: Sit.

[MATTY *pushes Deek into a sitting position and gives him the bit of sandwich. The others jeer.* MATTY *strokes Deek as the kids talk.*]

KERRY: Who's coming to the footy club dance?

MATTY: How much are the tickets?

BUDDAH: Ten dollars. It's a pig on a stick.

MATTY: Ten dollars? No.

TERRY: Your dad's got to be there. He plays in the back pocket for them.

MATTY: It'd be thirty dollars. He hasn't got it.

TERRY: Is it the same band as last year?

KERRY: Yeah.

TERRY: Aw, that singer, Claudine.

KERRY: Aw yeah. Like Dolly Parton.

BUDDAH: Was that a wig she was wearing?

TERRY: No. It was real.

KERRY: Ding dong, nobody has hair like that.

TERRY: Dolly Parton has.

KERRY: Those are wigs, dent.

TERRY: Yeah? Doesn't matter. Aw, Claudine.

MATTY: She's old. She's got lines here.

TERRY: I don't care.

KERRY: What was the song?

TERRY: Aw yeah. Em ... [*Singing with actions*]
        If I said you had a beautiful body
        Would you hold it against me?

KERRY: Aw yeah!

TERRY: I'm going. I'll get ten dollars.

MATTY: Are you in love with her, Turbo Tongue?

TERRY: Not really.

[*Deek starts barking at something. They turn to see what it is. He continues to bark over the following.*]

MATTY: What's the matter, Deek?

KERRY: Hey look. On the oval!

TERRY: Roos! Look at them.

MATTY: They must be starving to come down here.

KERRY: Well, they're not eating our footy field. Come on.

[*Much noise of agreement. Led by Deek, they run, then freeze.*]

SINGERS: So Year Five spent the recess
            Chasing starving roos,
            And in the days that follow
            Mobs of emus too.

            Roos came south in hundreds,
            No more than bags of bones,
            Seeking out the green grass
            But finding dirt and stones.

[*There is a music break during which the kids exit and* MR WALCH *drags on a sheep for shearing.*]

            Now shearing time has come around,
            The sheds are full of noise,
            And Matilda serves the stubbies
            For the sweating shearing boys.

            The sheep can hardly stand
            And their meat ain't worth a cent,
            But the fleece'll still fetch ten bucks,
            So get those backs a-bent.

WALCH: Matilda, would you like to get me a new set of blades from that bag of mine?

MATTY: [*off*] No worries, Mr Walch.

WALCH: [*to the sheep*] Come on, behave yourself.

[WALCH *gets the sheep in a headlock and starts to shear. The sheep does the sound of the electric shears. He does this for several moments, swearing at the sheep if it causes him trouble.* MR BELL *enters.*]

DAD: Sorry I'm late, Pete.

WALCH: No worries.

DAD: I had to queue all night at Katunga for orange peel and grape stalks.

WALCH: D'you get some?

DAD: [*getting his own sheep out of the pen*] I got enough for a couple of days. How are you going?

WALCH: Aw, good. Three of them died this morning, soon as the wool was off. Just wouldn't get up.

DAD: Yeah.

[*The two men shear through the following. Their sentences come quite slowly.*]

WALCH: What are you going to do with them, Ben?

DAD: I met a man in Katunga. He's going to agist them.

WALCH: Aw yeah?

[MATTY *enters.*]

MATTY: Your new blades, Mr Walch.

WALCH: I'm obliged, Matilda.

[MATTY *sets them down.*]

DAD: She's not talking to me.

WALCH: Oh?

DAD: She was having a nice tea last week and then asks ... [*To* MATTY] What did you call that lamb you were getting so attached to?

MATTY: 'Snowy'.

DAD: Asked where Snowy was. I said, 'Well, Snowy's somewhere between your gullet and your stomach'.

MATTY: You better not kill Cottontop, Dad.

DAD: Way things are going I won't have to.

WALCH: Matilda, I heard your little basketball team beat Katunga Saturday.

MATTY: Aw yeah, Mr Walch. Fifty-three to forty-eight. We're second now.

WALCH: Good.

MATTY: And we're got Taterloo last game of the season.

WALCH: Are you going to the dance?

MATTY: I don't know. Are we, Dad?

DAD: Can't afford it this year. Matilda, would you go and help your mother with that orange peel?

MATTY: Can I drive the tractor, Dad?

DAD: Ask your mother. And don't tell her I said you could drive it.

[MATTY *heads off.*]

MATTY: Awww.

[*She exits. Pause.* WALCH *finishes off his sheep, leads it off and starts to change his blades while* DAD *continues.*]

DAD: How are your fingers, Pete?

WALCH: No worries. Yours?

DAD: Well, keep it to yourself, but I reckon this arthritis is going to give me a couple of years of this at the most.

WALCH: Yeah. How's the bank treating you?

DAD: They'll have me wool cheque, but that's all they'll get this year. Can't last much longer, I reckon.

WALCH: You'll come through. You're a good farmer.

DAD: I don't know about that any more.

[DAD *finishes shearing his sheep and pushes it away. It staggers a few paces, then falls. It tries to rise. It falls back again. It twitches.* WALCH *and* DAD *watch. It twitches more. Then the sheep dies.* DAD *shakes his head. Pause. They both automatically grab an end each and cart it off. Music.*]

MATTY: [*off*] Mum! Mum!

[MATTY *enters.*]

MUM: [*off*] Yes?

MATTY: Will you and Dad play Monopoly with me?

MUM: [*off*] When we've finished the dishes. You set out the board.

MATTY: Aw yeah.

[*Spot the dog enters.*]

[*Whispering*] Spot, how'd you get in here? Aw, you want to be in front of the fire, don't you? Well, just stay out of sight. Go on.

[*She gives Spot a shove and he moves off.* MATTY *sets up the imaginary Monopoly board.*]

I'm going to get Mayfair and Park Lane tonight, no worries. I'm not letting Mum get them again. Chance. Community Chest. And a thousand dollars.

[DAD *enters.*]

DAD: [*to Spot*] Out!

MATTY: Aw, Dad.

DAD: Out, Spot. Don't look at Matilda. Out!
  [*The dog leaves mournfully.*]
MATTY: Dad, what are you dressed up for?
  [MUM *enters.*]
MUM: It's Saturday night, isn't it?
MATTY: You're dressed up too, Mum. What - ?
DAD: I heard there was a footy dance on tonight.
MATTY: But we're not going. You said -
MUM: Show her the tickets, Ben.
MATTY: Awww.
  [MATTY *is suddenly happy and excited.*]
  Aw, but I can't dance.
MUM: You can do the slowies.
MATTY: Yeah, but I want to do the fast ones.
MUM: What's the time, Ben?
DAD: It won't start for an hour.
MUM: Well, teach her. You're a good dancer.
DAD: Aw when? Awright. What's that song they play at the
  finish? It's on their tape. We've got it somewhere.
MUM: I'll get it.
DAD: Yeah, they play it after the raffle. The fat one with the
  beard, always makes the same joke at the raffle. First prize
  one week in the city. Second prize two weeks in the city.
MUM: I'll put it on.
DAD: Well Matilda, can I have the pleasure of this dance?
MATTY: Aw yeah Dad.
  [MUM *inserts the tape. The singers do the song 'Road to
  Gundagai'.* MUM *and* DAD *might join in while he teaches*
  MATTY *the steps. After a while, encouraged by her dad,*
  MATTY *gets the hang of it. The phone rings.* MUM *turns
  off the tape.*]
MUM: I wonder who that is. The man from Katunga who's
  going to take your sheep?
DAD: [*moving to the phone*] No, he's let me down. He won't
  take them. I think I know who it is.
  [*The phone is played by the arm of an actor.*]
  Hello ... Oh Kev. You got my message. Matilda, come
  and say 'Hello' to your Uncle Kev, and then go and wait
  for us in the ute.
MATTY: Why Dad?

[*She takes the phone.*]

Hello Uncle Kev. How's the city? ... Are you coming up to see us? ... Drive up in your cab ... Yeah ... Awright ... 'Bye.

[DAD *takes the phone.*]

Why do I have to go and sit in the ute, Dad?

DAD: [*into the phone*] Hello Kev.

[*He waves* MATTY *away. She goes.*]

No, I haven't told Matilda.

[*Pause.*]

I've got to shoot them tomorrow. The man that was going to take them has let me down. And that's the end of it, Kev ... Yeah ... We're moving to the city. [*To* MUM] Is she gone?

MUM: Yeah.

DAD: I need a job, Kev. Yeah. Yeah, I read about G.M.H. in the papers, but that's not the only factory in the city. Well, can you ask around? ... Yeah ... I'll do anything as long as it pays ... Thanks, Kev ... Yeah ... G'bye.

[*He puts the phone down.* MUM *goes to him.*]

MUM: When are you going to tell her? Or shall I?

DAD: I'll tell her tomorrow.

MUM: Poor kid.

DAD: Yeah. Well, let's go and enjoy ourselves, shall we?

MUM: Yeah.

[*They go. The singers repeat one verse of 'Road to Gundagai'. The music continues, followed by shots. Two sheep enter, digging for food with their feet. There are more shots. The sheep look up as if they know what is going to happen, then return to foraging.* DAD *and* MATTY *enter with a gun.* MATTY *hangs back.* DAD *goes forward and shoots each of the sheep. Pause. He waits, then kicks the sheep.*]

MATTY: Dad, it'll be awright. Next year.

DAD: Matilda?

MATTY: Yeah, Dad?

DAD: I've got to tell you something.

MATTY: Yeah, Dad?

DAD: There isn't going to be a next year.

MATTY: What?

DAD: Not here, anyway.

MATTY: What?

DAD: Look around you. The wind's taken the topsoil off this paddock and blown it all over Australia. Left us with stones. It's finished. We're moving.

MATTY: Moving?

DAD: Yeah.

MATTY: Moving? Moving? But we live here, Dad. What? Aw, no. Where? It'll rain. Katunga?

DAD: No. Not Katunga. Only job I could have got there was the tractor place, and that's closing.

MATTY: Not Katunga? Where, Dad? Where?

DAD: The city. We're all moving to the city.

MATTY: The where?

DAD: I told you.

MATTY: The city? But we don't know anyone in the city.

DAD: We know your Uncle Kev.

MATTY: He's old.

DAD: He's my age. It can't be helped.

MATTY: But what about school?

DAD: There's schools in the city.

MATTY: What about the team? We're playing Taterloo in two weeks.

DAD: They'll still win it.

MATTY: Awww. Who's going to play in the back pocket next season?

DAD: They'll find someone else.

MATTY: No, Dad. My friends are here. I don't know anybody there.

DAD: You'll make new friends.

MATTY: I won't. I won't. I can't.

DAD: You will!

MATTY: What about Kerry and Buddah and ... ? Are they coming?

DAD: Don't be stupid, Matilda. Of course they're not coming.

MATTY: What about Spot? Is he coming?

DAD: No, Spot won't be coming.

MATTY: You're going to shoot him, aren't you, Dad?

   [MUM *enters.* MATTY *runs to her.*]

   Mum, Dad says we're moving. Tell him we're not.

MUM: We've got to, Matilda.

MATTY: Awww no. No.

MUM: Do you think your father'd be doing this if he had any choice? He's been queuing up for orange peel night after night in Katunga to keep these alive. Sheep that aren't worth a cent at the sales. He's done his best.

MATTY: It'll rain. I'm not going. I'm not.

DAD: I'm not arguing with you, Matilda. We're all going. Come on, Mum, we'd best go and pack.

MATTY: I'm not.

[*They go.*]

I'm not. I'm staying here. I'm not going to the city. I'm not.

[*She starts to cry.*]

SINGER: That land that hadn't seen no rain
            For nigh on a full year
            Was flooded now from Matty's eyes
            With great salt bitter tears.

            She could feel her heart a-beating,
            It was pounding like a train.
            There was shaking in her knees
            And fear inside her brain.

[MATTY *hangs her head as* MUM *and* DAD *enter with real, battered suitcases. They place them at the front of the stage and go.*]

            Was this the last time she would see
            The farm where she was born?
            Last time to feed the chooks and lambs
            And loose the dogs at dawn?

            Last time to swim in summer dams
            And splash brown water white?
            Last time to gather up the traps
            And go bunnying at night?

[MUM *and* DAD *re-enter and put down real cardboard boxes of* MATTY's *toys: teddy bears and basket ball, etcetera. The toys are well-used and colourful. These and the suitcases are the only real props in the play, with the exception of the paper boat at the end.*]

MATTY: No!

[*Her parents go.*]

SINGER: Matty closed her eyes and in her mind
            She saw the city there,
            The cars and trucks in thousands
            And people everywhere.

            No horizon could she see
            That goes on for miles and miles,
            Just buildings and tall towers
            That block out half the skies.

[*Music. Spot enters.* MATTY *holds him, head against head.*]
            And in that picture in her head
            Of that city far away
            She didn't see a single face
            She knew in any way.

            A thousand strangers passed her by;
            Not one of them she knew.
            Every face was strange to her,
            Every face was new.

MATTY: Dad? Mum? No.

[*Blackout on all but the singer.*]

SINGER: Well, that's the first part of the story, and it looks
like Matilda's got to go to the city, however she feels about
it. Whether the city's as bad as she thinks ... Well, we'll
be showing you what happens to Matilda in the city in about
ten minutes' time. So we'll see you than, awright?

[*The music plays out and all exit.*]

END OF ACT ONE

ACT TWO

The actors enter the auditorium with a wave.

ALL: G'day again.

> [*They take the response.* DAD *and* MUM *take their positions in the ute.* MATTY *stands some way off.*]

SINGER: Well, if you're all comfortable we'll go with Matilda on her journey to the city and see what happens to her. Part Two. 'The Ballad of Matilda in the City', and it goes something like this.

> [*Music.*]

DAD: Come on Matilda, time to go!

MATTY: Spot!

> [*Music.* MATTY, *looking back, comes forward to the ute.* MUM *opens the door to appropriate sound effects and gets out.* MATTY *gets in between them.* MUM *gets in and the door closes. The music continues as* DAD *turns over the engine and does the effects as it coughs, then coughs again.*]

SINGERS:　　That old ute that smelt of super
　　　　　　And chooks and sheep as well
　　　　　　Is hosed down with bore water now
　　　　　　And's lost that country smell.

　　　　　　It's loaded high with Matty's toys
　　　　　　And a thousand memories
　　　　　　As the three of them set off
　　　　　　For that city by the sea.

> [*The music continues.* DAD *coughs again.*]

DAD: Brmmm. Brmmm. Brmmm-mmm-mmm.

MATTY: Cheer up, Matilda! It's going to be alright. Mum!

SINGERS:　　Matty between her dad and mum;
　　　　　　Her tears are making pools,
　　　　　　And she cries some more as they pass the door
　　　　　　Of the Yorktown Area School.

MATTY: Dingo! Buddah! Dingo!

SINGERS: In the yard her mates are playing,
             But they do not hear her roar.
             It was then the pain started up again:
             She would see them nevermore.

  [*Speaking*]
             Charlie over the water,
             Charlie over the sea.
             Charlie broke a teapot
             And blamed it onto me.

DAD: Brmmm-mmm-mmm.
MUM: Matilda, d'you want a sandwich?
    [MATTY *shakes her head.*]
  They're your favourite.
    [MATTY *shakes her head.*]
SINGERS: To the front the green sign on the road
             Says the city's name in white;
             Six hundred and fifty kilometres
             And they'll be there tonight.

             But Matty looks back at her home
             Till it becomes a dot ...
             Goodbye, Dingo and Buddah ...

  [*The music continues.*]
MATTY: [*to herself*] Turbo Tongue, Deek, Dingo!
    [*Pause. Music.*]
SINGERS: Goodbye Spot.

MUM: It's going to be alright, Matilda. I promise.
    [MUM *puts an arm around her.*]
DAD: Yeah. Brmmm-mmm-mmm.
SINGERS: The kilometres, they fly by
             On that highway to the sea
             Where the riders of the long paddocks
             Are grazing sheep for free.

             The bush, it fades away now as
             The day gives up its light
             And suddenly below them
             Is the city in the night.

[*Coloured lights flash accompanied by traffic noises made by the singers, followed by shouting voices running over one another. They need not be distinct.*]

FIRST VOICE: Can't you read that sign?

SECOND VOICE: *Sun* and *Globe.*

[*The* THIRD VOICE *does a car horn.*]

THIRD VOICE: Hey!

FIRST VOICE: 'No thongs.'

THIRD VOICE: Hey, you, Nunga!

SECOND VOICE: *Sun* and *Globe.*

[*The* THIRD VOICE *does another car horn.*]

MUM: D'you know the way, Ben?

DAD: Kev sent me a map. Read it out to me.

[*The noises continue.*]

MUM: Is this Main Street?

DAD: I don't know.

MUM: Matilda, we're looking for Ryan Road.

[*The voices slip into a mixture of Italian, Croat and Vietnamese, again all running into each other.*]

There it is. What number?

DAD: Forty-eight. He's left me the key. He's going to be out in his cab till midnight. He said to make ourselves at home.

MUM: Here it is.

[DAD *brings the ute to a halt.*]

It's a nice little house, Matilda.

MATTY: They're so close.

[MUM *opens the door of the ute and they get out.*]

DAD: Awright, Matilda, it's late. Your Uncle Kev's made up a room in the back for you, so I think you'd better get straight to bed. We'll bring the cases in.

MUM: I'll come and see you when we're unloaded.

DAD: Cheer up!

[MATTY *goes back and off.*]

[*Shouting after her*] And don't forget your prayers, Matilda. Come on, let's get this stuff into the house. It's awright, isn't it?

[*They look at it.* MUM *nods. They go. The street noises continue.* MATTY *enters and climbs into bed. She listens to the sounds of the street, then prays.*]

MATTY: As I lay me down to sleep I pray the Lord my soul to keep.
[*Pause.*]
Jesus, can you see me? This is my new address and it's horrible, Jesus. It's Uncle Kev's C.B. room, looks like. There's horrible flowers on the wall and pictures of a fat old bloke called ... [*Looking at the wall*] 'Elvis'. Listen, Jesus, you can hear the people in the next house.
[*Pause.*]
They don't even speak English. And the cars. Jesus, don't let Dad get a job here; then we'll have to go back home. Please!

MUM: [*off*] Matilda! Matilda!

MATTY: [*to Jesus, finishing off*] Please!
[MUM *enters.*]

MUM: Good news, Matilda!

MATTY: What? Are we going home?

MUM: Matilda, will you stop that? No. Your Uncle Kev's left a note. You know he's got his own cab now. City Super Cabs. Those were the blue ones we saw in the city centre. Well, your Uncle Kev drives it in the daytime and this bloke, Gino, drives it at night. Well, this Gino says he don't want to do it any more after the end of the month, so if your Uncle Kev can teach your dad the city streets, your dad can do the night driving.

MATTY: Awww.

MUM: Isn't that good news?

MATTY: Can I go with Dad when he goes driving?

MUM: I've brought in your toys so you've got your friends around you.

MATTY: Mum, can I? I drove with him at home.

MUM: Matilda, this is your home now, awright? And no you can't.
[*Pause.*]
[*Softening*] You can't. Your Dad'll be driving round in the cab taking city people to where they want to go. They sit in the front seat if they want to. You can't be sitting there.

MATTY: I could go in the back.

MUM: No. The cab company wouldn't let you.

MATTY: I sat with him on the tractor. In the ute ...

MUM: That's different, Matilda. It's different here.

MATTY: How long'll Dad be out driving?

MUM: Well, according to your Uncle Kev, it's hard making a living from a cab. I don't know. Eleven or twelve hours.

MATTY: That's ... I'll never see him!

MUM: You'll see him on his day off. We'll go to the sea.

MATTY: I want to go with him.

MUM: Well, you can't. You couldn't at night anyway. You need to sleep. Be fresh for your new school. There's a nice school down the road. There's about eight hundred children go there.

MATTY: How many?

MUM: About eight hundred.

MATTY: Eight hundred?

MUM: Yeah, it'll be a bit different at first, but there's sure to be lots of friends you can make there. I'm going to take you next week.

MATTY: I don't want to go.

MUM: Well you are going! You've got to.

MATTY: Can't I stay with you, Mum?

MUM: No, dear. I'll be working too. If I can find a job.

MATTY: Who's going to be here when I get back, Mum?

MUM: I won't be long after you. You'll have a key.

MATTY: Key?

MUM: Yeah. [*Getting up*] They lock things up in the city, Matilda. There's a lot of five-finger discount in the city. Now get some sleep. G'night.

MATTY: Mum!

MUM: G'night, Matilda.

MATTY: Mum!

[MUM *goes.*]

Awww.

SINGER: Waltzing Matilda, waltzing Matilda,
You'll come a-waltzing, Matilda, with me ...

SINGERS: M'tilda stares up at the ceiling
As the car lights come and go,
Moving like the searchlights
In a World War movie show.

> Staring at the patterns on
> The wall for hours and hours,
> She makes out cruel faces in
> The leaves and in the flowers.

[*The music continues.*]

MATTY: Mum! Mum!

    [*Pause.*]

    Dad! Dad!

SINGERS: Her mummy didn't love her,
> Nor could her daddy too,
> To bring her to this far-off town
> Where everything was new.

> And Jesus had just shut his ears
> To everything she said,
> So Matty closes up her eyes
> And wishes she was dead.

[*The music continues.*]

MATTY: Awww.

DAD: [*off*] Matilda, go to sleep! We'll have a talk in the morning.

    [*Pause.*]

MATTY: [*to herself*] We won't. We won't.

SINGERS: Her mind is like the dust storms
> They had had all year,
> But one idea just grows and grows
> And now it's very clear.

[*The music slows.* MATTY *is determined, confused and frightened.*]

[*Speaking*]

> She wouldn't speak a single word
> From tomorrow, never, never.
> Matty shuts her lips up tight
> For ever and for ever.

[*A musical discord. Blackout. Pause.*]

DAD: Come on! Test me again. It's like I was back in school. [*Lights up.* MATTY *lies in bed as she was.* DAD *and* MUM *sit together in the next room.*]

MUM: I'll just go and see if Matilda's up.

DAD: Leave her. She'll get over it.

MUM: I can't leave her. It's her first day at school. And she'd better get over it today. Three days and she hasn't said a word to either of us!

DAD: It takes time. One more question.

MUM: Awright. I'm getting in your cab at the railway station.

DAD: Awright. Yes, Madam, where would you like to go?

MUM: I'd like to go to the airport.

DAD: International? Or domestic?

MUM: International.

DAD: Right. Airport? I've done this before. Aw yeah. Right. I go up King Street to Maitland. Turn right. Four blocks and then left onto Moore Street. Up to the fork and take the left and I'm on the freeway. And there are sign posts all the way. There you are, Madam, the airport.

MUM: Very good, Ben. [*Shouting*] Matilda! School!

    [MATTY *starts to get out of bed and get ready.*]

DAD: You think I'll make a cab driver?

MUM: Yeah. Matilda! How are you feeling, Ben?

DAD: The city. I'm getting used to it.

MUM: Ben!

DAD: Awright. I will do. Got to. Why's everyone in such a hurry?

MUM: Yeah.

DAD: And shouting things at you. 'Hick.' 'Shit shoveller.' Do I smell or something?

MUM: No.

DAD: Feel like hitting them.

MUM: Well, don't.

    [MATTY *enters.*]

    There's your breakfast, Matilda.

    [MATTY *shakes her head slightly.*]

DAD: G'day, Matilda.

    [*Silence.*]

MUM: Your dad said 'G'day', Matilda.

DAD: It's awright. Look, Matilda, you don't have to say anything to me, but this is a big day for you. A new school. Try and mix in. Yeah. We're trying. I know it'll be hard.

MUM: It's hard for us too, you know.

    [*Silence.*]

DAD: [*to* MUM] I'll pick you up outside the school in about half an hour. We'll go and see about this job of yours, if you're still insisting on it.

MUM: Come on, Matilda. [*To* DAD] Yes I am. I'm not sitting around here all day.

DAD: Awright.

[DAD *goes.* MUM *looks at* MATTY, *then holds out her hand.*]

MUM: Are you ready, Matilda?

[MATTY *ignores the hand and goes.* MUM *follows. Playground noises fade in, followed by a bell.* BINH, *a Vietnamese girl, enters. She sits up high and watches.*]

FIRST VOICE: [*off*] Hey Marco, you done the homework?

SECOND VOICE: Do your own.

FIRST VOICE: Awww. Hey, Kelly! Have you done the homework?

[*Two boys,* LINDSAY *and* DAVID, *enter playing mimed basketball.* LINDSAY *looks with hostility at* BINH.]

LINDSAY: How many more chinks are they letting in this school?

DAVID: She's Vietnamese. Leave her alone. She's not doing nothing.

LINDSAY: Well they can do nothing somewhere else. Catch.

[*He throws the imaginary ball to* DAVID *and takes something from his pocket. He mimes writing in big letters.*]

DAVID: What are you doing?

LINDSAY: Decorating.

DAVID: That's far out. 'Boat peopple go home.' There's only two Ps in 'people', ding dong.

LINDSAY: [*to the girl*] Understand?

DAVID: She can't speak English, so you won't be able to read it. [*Throwing the ball*] Come on. [*To the girl*] You want a game?

BINH: *Toi khong hieu.* [*'I don't understand.'*]

LINDSAY: She's not playing.

[LINDSAY *dribbles up to* DAVID, *around him and shoots.*] Aw yeah.

[*Pause.* DAVID *gets the ball.*]

[*Moving towards* BINH] If she wants to be an Australian I could help her.

DAVID: Leave her.

LINDSAY: [*to* BINH] Lesson One. Cricket. You play cricket in Vietnam, do you?

DAVID: She can't understand you!

LINDSAY: Awright, chink, you've got a bowler and a wicket-keeper, so now you want to set your field ...

DAVID: Lindsay!

BINH: *Xin loi, toi khong hieu ban noi gi.* [*'I'm sorry, I don't understand what you're talking about.'*]

DAVID: Lins!

LINDSAY: Now you've got a choice. [*Quickly*] Over here you can have a fine leg, a square leg, silly mid on, mid on, long on and mid wicket.

DAVID: [*throwing the ball to him*] Come on!

[*During the following,* MATTY *and* MUM *enter.*]

LINDSAY: [*throwing the ball back*] Then on this side you can have a long off, mid off, silly mid off, extra cover, cover, cover point, gully, fifth slip, fourth slip, third slip, second slip, first slip and third man. It's up to you.

DAVID: Lins!

LINDSAY: [*to* BINH] You heard of Alan Border?

[DAVID *notices* MATTY.]

DAVID: Alright, if you don't want to play, I'll play with someone else. Hey shorty, catch!

[MATTY *moves away slightly so that* DAVID *doesn't throw it.*]

MUM: Catch it, Matilda. [*To* DAVID] She's shy.

LINDSAY: [*to* BINH] Alan Border.

DAVID: [*to* MATTY] You play?

MUM: It's Matilda. First day. Which is Mr McKay's class?

DAVID: There! He's awright.

[MUM *and* MATTY *move towards* BINH.]

BINH: [*to* LINDSAY] You Alan Border?

LINDSAY: [*moving away*] She's a moron. [*To* DAVID] Here!

[DAVID *turns and throws the ball.*]

She thinks *I'm* Alan Border. [*Dribbling the ball*] Who was that?

DAVID: Matilda something.

LINDSAY: [*looking her over*] Another nunga. Come on!

[*They continue to play.* BINH *watches* MATTY *as they approach. The players freeze.*]

MUM: G'day.

BINH: G'day.

MUM: Matilda. First day.

[BINH *doesn't understand a word.*]

There are a lot of foreigners here. But I bet there'll be lots of Australians as well.

[*The bell goes.* BINH *heads off.*]

Right, now, Matilda, there's your new classroom. You get in there and make some friends. Matilda?

[*Silence.* MATTY *pulls away.*]

Matilda, in a couple of minutes this Mr McKay is going to ask you to answer your name. You'll have to say something then.

[*The bell continues.* DAVID *runs off, into class.*]

Now in you go. [*Turning to go*] I'll see you tonight.

[MUM *goes.* MATTY *just stands there, then starts slowly to move off after the others.* LINDSAY *enters, running. She is in his way.*]

LINDSAY: Hey, Nunga.

[*Pause.*]

After me. After me.

[*She stops. He goes off. The bell continues. She follows. Pause.* BINH *enters the classroom, followed by* LINDSAY. *They get seated. Then* MATTY *enters. She is standing when* MR McKAY *enters.*]

McKAY: Are you Matilda? Sit anywhere you like, Matilda.

[*She sits.*]

Good morning, class.

BINH: ⎫
LINDSAY: ⎬ [*together*] Good morning, Mr McKay.

McKAY: Lindsay O'Keefe, do you want to go home to Ireland?

LINDSAY: What, sir?

McKAY: I was watching you writing on the school wall, Lindsay. 'Boat peopple go home.' One P in 'people', by the way, Lindsay.

LINDSAY: Sir, I ...

McKAY: What do you think your grandad and grandma came to Australia in, Lindsay?

LINDSAY: Emmm ... A boat, sir.

McKAY: Yes. So did mine, Lindsay. And most of the grandparents of this class, I should think.

LINDSAY: Yeah, but we live here now, sir.

McKAY: Quite so. And so do these Vietnamese children, Lindsay, awright? So at recess, would you be so good as to rub that nonsense off the school wall, Lindsay? Thank you.

LINDSAY: Sir.

McKAY: Good. Well, we're having lots of new faces this term, aren't we? [*Touching* BINH *on the shoulder*] Are you settling in, Binh?

[BINH *smiles.*]

And it's a welcome today for Matilda Bell from Yorktown. Is that right, Matilda? Just arrived in the city. Well, anything you're worried about, Matilda, you just come and ask. Now, roll. Everyone here? Lindsay ...

LINDSAY: Sir.

McKAY: Binh?

BINH: Sir.

McKAY: I'll put your name at the bottom, Matilda. Awright? Matilda Bell?

[*Pause.*]

Matilda? You had a roll call in your area school, didn't you? Just say 'sir', alright? Matilda Bell?

[*Pause.*]

Alright, Lindsay, that's enough. Matilda doesn't need your help. Matilda? Lindsay! Awright, Matilda, take your time. No worries. We'll try again tomorrow. Right, Lindsay's favourite subject. Spelling. Open your books at page fifteen. Awright? Page fifteen.

[*Blackout. The lights fade up on the school playground at recess. The bell goes again. Then* LINDSAY *enters, laughing and bouncing the imaginary ball.* MATTY *enters and he laughs again.*]

LINDSAY: You ever seen anything like it? You ever seen anything like it?

[DAVID *enters.*]

DAVID: What?

LINDSAY: That hick. Can't even answer her name on the roll. 'Matilda Bell?' Nothing. And then he starts on me. 'Lindsay, that's enough. Matilda doesn't need your help.'

DAVID: Let's play.

LINDSAY: She's just a stupid nunga.

DAVID: I'll defend. [*To* MATTY] Want a game?

    [*She turns away and sits down.*]

LINDSAY: You're wasting your time. She's a dummy. The
cat got her tongue or something.

DAVID: Just 'cause she won't answer the roll don't mean she
won't talk to us. Matilda, do you want a game?

    [*Again no response.*]

LINDSAY: Come on! She's a waste of time.

    [*The two boys play. They freeze as* BINH *comes out. She
sits near* MATTY.]

BINH: G'day.

    [*Pause. No answer.*]

    Toi la Binh. Toi tu Da-Nang o Vietnam. ['*I am Binh. I'm
from Da-Nang in Vietnam.*']

    [MATTY *gets up and sits somewhere else. The play resumes.*]

DAVID: What a shot!

    [*The ball rolls near* MATTY.]

LINDSAY: Get it, Dave!

DAVID: [*to* MATTY] Hey pass the ball back, will you?

LINDSAY: Quickly!

    [DAVID *holds out his hand.* MATTY *picks up the ball, and
for a second there might be a connection between them.
Then she gives the ball a giant boot over both their heads.
They watch it fly over with amazement.*]

    [*Moving towards* MATTY] I don't believe it.

DAVID: Hey! Watch it. McKay's watching.

LINDSAY: Where?

DAVID: There. [*To* MATTY] What did you do that for, you little
hick?

LINDSAY: That's gone out in the street, you little moron. Now
go and get it!

    [MATTY *stands up to them, fists clenched by her side.*]

DAVID: Forget it. I'll go and get it.

LINDSAY: She's going to get it!

DAVID: I'll get it.

    [DAVID *goes.*]

LINDSAY: That's your last chance, nunga.

    [LINDSAY *goes.* BINH *watches* MATTY. *Music. Blackout.*]

DAD: I'm not shouting.

MUM: You're shouting.

DAD: I'm not shouting!

MUM: You're shouting, Ben.

[*The lights fade up on* MATTY, DAD *and* MUM.]

DAD: Alright, I'm shouting! Right, I'll try again. Now, is this quiet enough for everyone? Matilda. Right? I've got the day off. I've been working twelve days straight learning these city streets so this family can be fed. And now Kev says, 'Take the day off'. The weather's fine and your mum and me feel like a break. We'd like to go somewhere. We'd like to go somewhere with you, Matilda. Now, where would you like to go? Would you like to go to the zoo?

[*Silence.*]

Would you like to go to the beach?

[*Silence.*]

Alright, you say where you would like to bloody go!

MUM: Ben!

[*A knock comes from off.*]

DAD: Now who the hell's that?

MUM: I'll go.

[DAD *and* MATTY *are left alone.*]

DAD: Matilda.

[*Pause.*]

Matilda, do you think we're having it easy? Listen, Matilda, if you can't think of us, think of your Uncle Kev. He's let us use his house. You're his favourite niece. No, how do you think he feels? You haven't spoken a word to him since we came to the city. He's bloody upset.

[*Pause.*]

Oh, go on. Go to your room.

[MATTY *goes.* DAD *shakes his head. Then* MUM *enters with* MR McKAY.]

MUM: Ben, this is Mr McKay from school.

DAD: Oh, come in, Mr McKay. Sorry the place is a bit ... My city maps. I'm learning to be a cab driver.

McKAY: Ah.

MUM: It's about Matilda.

DAD: Yeah. Well ... do you want us to go and fetch Matilda, Mr McKay?

McKAY: No, I don't think so. No, I just wanted to have a word with you. You see, to be honest, I don't know what to do. We get lots of kids coming to the school from interstate, from the bush, from abroad. It takes a while for them to settle in. That's natural. It's hard. But after three weeks Matilda still hasn't said a word to anybody.

DAD: Yeah. I know.

McKAY: She's upsetting the other kids and they're laughing at her. Making jokes. It's getting pretty bad, Mrs Bell. I had to haul one boy off who was going to punch her head if she didn't talk. I just thought maybe you could tell me what was going on in her head, because I don't know.

DAD: It's the city, I reckon. She's always had a mind of her own.

MUM: She blames us for bringing her here.

DAD: We've had nothing out of her since the day we arrived.

MUM: Could you just try and be patient with her?

McKAY: I'll try, but -

DAD: [*interrupting, to* MUM] She's disrupting the class. That right, Mr McKay?

McKAY: Yeah.

MUM: We'll have another talk with her. See if we can get anywhere.

McKAY: Good. Good.

[McKAY *moves toward the door.*]

MUM: Sorry to cause you all this trouble.

McKAY: No worries.

DAD: Yeah. Thanks.

[McKAY *goes. They look at each other.*]

MUM: Matilda!

DAD: Listen, I've got a couple of things I should be doing on the cab and I'm mad enough to say something I'll be sorry about. You talk to her, will you?

MUM: Alright. Matilda!

DAD: I'll be in the garage. Don't shout at her.

[*He goes.*]

MUM: Matilda!

[*She walks back and forth and* MATTY *enters.*]

Sit down, please, Matilda.

[MATTY *does so.*]

Now, young lady, you and me are going to have a little talk and I'm not doing all the talking. Awright?

[*Silence.*]

Awright. I've got all night. Now I know you didn't want to come to the city, Matilda. Nor did your dad and me. But we're trying to make the best of it. Don't you think we're doing our best? Matilda?

[*Silence.*]

Oh, sometimes I could ...

[*Pause.*]

Your school teacher's been round. Says the kids are all laughing at you. Seems like you want everyone to hate you. Do you? Do you?

[*Silence.*]

Can't you tell me what's wrong, Matilda?

[*Silence.*]

Look, there's kids out there in the street in front of the house. You could just walk out there and start playing with them.

[*Silence.*]

Listen, Matilda, I can't go on like this. I'm not sleeping.

[*Silence.*]

You're a selfish little girl ... No, I don't mean ... Matilda, we're getting out of debt here. We're staying. It's hard enough ... The way you're behaving, it's impossible. Thank you very much, Matilda!

[*She turns away. Pause.* MATTY *is now very upset and almost moves to her mother. She feels guilt at how upset her mother is, but she can't bring herself to help.* MATTY *bursts into silent tears and runs off.* MUM *is unaware that* MATTY *has gone. She turns around and is puzzled. A suspicion creeps into her mind. She goes to one side. No one there. She runs to the other side.*]

[*Shouting*] Matilda! Matilda! Ben! Ben!

[DAD *enters.*]

Ben!

DAD: What's the matter?

MUM: Matilda's run away.

DAD: Get in the cab.

[*They go to the cab and get in.*]

Which way? Brmmm.

MUM: I don't know.

> [DAD's *call sign comes over the* RADIO. *He picks up an imaginary receiver.*]

DAD: Oh, no.

RADIO: Car Ten forty-two, can you go to the railway station?

DAD: Listen, mate, I can't go anywhere. My little daughter's run away.

RADIO: Awww. Best of luck, mate.

DAD: Thanks. Brmmm-mmm-mmm.

> [*The lights crossfade from* DAD *and* MUM *to* MATTY *running. The city noises are very loud. A heartbeat drums away.*]

SINGERS: Matty ran out on the street
            And she ran far into the night.
            The city sparkles round her like
            A giant rainbow light.

            The juke boxes were playing
            Songs about some broken heart.
            They couldn't tell Matilda Bell's
            Was breaking clean apart.

> [*The lights crossfade back to the cab.*]

MUM: Aw, Ben.

DAD: We'll find her.

> [*The call sign comes over the* RADIO *again.* DAD *picks it up.*]

RADIO: Listen, driver, that little girl of yours? Give me a description and I'll give it out to all the other cab drivers in the city.

DAD: Aw, that's good of you, mate. Aw, I don't know how to describe her to you.

MUM: [*grabbing the mike*] Give me that. She's wearing white shoes and her clothes are blue. She's about four feet tall and yellow hair and she doesn't speak.

RADIO: No worries. We'll find her.

MUM: Thanks. Bless you. Bless you.

DAD: Yeah. Thanks, mate.

> [*The lights crossfade to* MATTY.]

SINGERS: Matty ran it seemed for ever,
                  Till her legs just wouldn't go,
                  And as the dawn came up
                  She was walking slow.

                  Her feet were torn, her brain was numb,
                  As tired as she could be,
                  When she saw a brilliant light
                  As the sun shone on the sea.

[*The music slows. The performers start to make the sound
of a gentle early-morning tide. The sound continues over
the following. Seagulls cry. She looks up as they wheel
overhead. Pause. Then she rolls up her trousers and walks
into the sea. She keeps watching the seagulls. The music
continues. She kicks water and then does it with her hands.
She stands and watches the sea. Voices come from far off.*]

DAVID: [*off*] Matilda! Matilda!

LINDSAY: [*off*] Matilda.

[*She half turns in their direction, then turns back. She
continues to shoo the water with her hands and watch the
birds. Then* DAVID *and* LINDSAY *enter, panting. The sound
of the tide gently fades away.*]

DAVID: Matilda!

[*She ignores them.*]

LINDSAY: She's psycho.

DAVID: Matilda.

LINDSAY: Out on the beach at six o'clock in the morning with
every cab driver in the city out looking for her ...

DAVID: Are you cold, Matilda?

LINDSAY: Hey, you want this footy jacket? I don't need it.
I've been running.

[*She ignores the offer.*]

[*To* DAVID] See what I mean? [*To* MATTY] Hey, listen: our
school's awright. You know? It's awright.

[BINH *follows* DAVID *and* LINDSAY *on.*]

[*To* BINH] I'm just saying: our school's awright, isn't it?

[BINH *gives no particular response.*]

[*To* MATTY] There y'are.

DAVID: Lins, have you got thirty cents?

LINDSAY: Yeah.

DAVID: [*to* BINH] Hi. [*To* MATTY] Listen, there's a phone on the pier. I'm going to phone into City Super Cabs and tell them we've found you. Awright? [*To* BINH] Don't let her run away.

LINDSAY: [*to* MATTY] And you're going to pay me back this thirty cents. Okay?

DAVID: Come on. Race you. [*Moving off*] Come on.

LINDSAY: I'm giving you a start.

DAVID: To that phone box? I don't need a start.

LINDSAY: Wanna bet?

DAVID: Yeah.

LINDSAY: Fifty cents.

DAVID: You're on. Go.

[*They run off. The seagulls cry out.* BINH *looks up at them.*]

BINH: [*pointing*] *Chim haiau. Chung toi cieng thay no o Vietnam.* [*'Seagulls. We see them in Vietnam.'*]

[*No answer. She also rolls up her trousers and comes into the sea. She looks at* MATTY. *Music. Then* BINH *takes a real square of coloured paper from her pocket and starts to make a boat out of it.* MATTY *tries hard not to look, but can't help glancing sideways. The waves lap.* BINH *finishes the boat and puts it down. She splashes it. They both look at it.*]

[*Conveying as much as possible through gesture*] *Toi vuot bien bang not chiec tau. Tu Da-Nang o Vietnam. Anh co biet Da-Nang khong? Tat ca gia dinh toi deu o tien tau. Den Singapore, roi vuot bien den Ma Lai, roi den Uc.* [*'I came across the sea in a boat. From Da-Nang in Vietnam. Have you heard of Da-Nang? All my family in one boat. To Singapore and then across the sea to Malaysia, then to Australia.'*] Near Darwin, Northern Territory. *Haim nguoi da o tien chice tau that nho do.* [*'Twenty people in that one small boat.'*]

[*She picks up the paper boat.*]

Do la cau chuyen cua toi. [*'This is me.'*]

[*She offers it to* MATTY. *No response.*]

Cam lay no. No danh cho ban. [*'Take it. It's for you.'*]

[*Pause. No response.* MATTY *turns away and wipes her eyes.* BINH *offers a handkerchief and is refused. She presses* MATTY, *who takes it and wipes her eyes without looking at*

BINH. *Pause.* MATTY *looks down at the boat. She shakes her head.* BINH *is puzzled.*]

BINH: Uh?

MATTY: Sink in five minutes.

BINH: Uh?

MATTY: That. Paper boat. Sink in five minutes.

BINH: Ah.

MATTY: What you want to use is yabby shells. Bottle top yabbies. Make good boats.

BINH: 'Yabby'?

MATTY: Yeah. Yabby.

[*She picks up the boat and inspects it.*]

BINH: 'Yabby'? Australian. Hard.

MATTY: Yeah? No worries.

BINH: 'No worries'?

MATTY: Yeah. No worries. It means ... well ... no worries. Do you play basketball?

BINH: 'Bask- ...'

MATTY: [*miming*] Basketball?

BINH: Oh? Basketball? *Vang, nguoi My da choi bong ro noi toi song khi ma toi bay loh nhu vay.* [*'Yes, the Americans played basketball where I lived when I was this high.*]

MATTY: You played basketball with Yanks? They're two metres twenty, some of them. Hey, are you any good? We could start a team at school.

BINH: [*pointing, in English*] Water.

MATTY: Yeah. It's the sea too.

BINH: 'Sea'?

MATTY: Yeah. Sea. Hey. [*Pointing*] Water. Sea. Right?
            Charlie over the water,
            Charlie over the sea.
            Charlie broke a teapot
            And blamed it onto me.

BINH: Charlie?

MATTY: Some bloke.

BINH: 'Teapot'?

    [MATTY *mimes a teapot.*]

  Ah. *Binh tia.* ['*Teapot.*']

MATTY: Come on then. 'Charlie ...'

BINH: 'Charlie over the ...'

MATTY: [*pointing*] 'Water ...'
BINH: Ah.

> Charlie over the sea.

BOTH:

> Charlie broke a teapot ...
> [*Pause.* BINH *shakes her head.*]

MATTY:

> And blamed it onto me.

Yeah. See?
MUM: [*off, shouting*] Matilda!
DAD: [*off, shouting*] Matilda!
MATTY: That's my mum and dad. [*Turning towards them*] I'm going to get it now.
BINH: 'Mum'. 'Dad'.
MATTY: Yeah.
MUM: [*off*] Matilda!
MATTY: Oh no.

> [MUM *and* DAD *enter angrily.*]

MUM: Matilda!
DAD: Now you come out of that water, young lady, and I'm going to tan your backside.
MUM: Oh Matilda, do you know what a night we've had? Hearing every traffic accident on the cab radio and thinking it might be you.
DAD: Your mum's been sick once. Well you can stay dumb as far as I'm concerned. I'm finished with you.
MATTY: Dad. Mum.

> [*Pause.*]

DAD: What?
MUM: She's talking.
DAD: [*to* MATTY] What did you -
MUM: [*interrupting*] She's talking. Matilda's talking.
MATTY: Dad, Mum, this is ... [*To* BINH] What's your name? You? Name?
BINH: 'Binh'.
MATTY: Binh. [*Holding up the paper boat*] She gave me this.
MUM: She's talking, Dad.
DAD: Well, about bloody time.

> [DAD *and* MUM *embrace.*]

Come here, Matilda.
[DAD *moves toward the sea.*]
MUM: Ben, your new shoes. They'll get wet.
DAD: Who cares?
MUM: I do. They cost forty-nine ninety-nine.
DAD: Awright.
[*He stops, takes off his shoes and rolls up his trousers.*]
Where's your new friend from, Matilda?
MATTY: Vietnam, Dad. How far away's that?
DAD: Oh, a long way.
MATTY: More than six hundred and fifty kilometres?
DAD: Aw yeah. More like six thousand. Across the sea.
[*He moves towards the sea again.*]
Come on, Mum.
MUM: I've never been in the sea before.
DAD: [*grabbing her hand*] Well, we're going in now.
[*They rush into the sea. They go up to* MATTY *and hug her.* BINH *turns away from this private moment.* MUM *looks over* MATTY'*s shoulder at the Vietnamese girl alone in the sea. Gently,* MUM *goes forward and puts her hand out. They shake.* DAD *follows suit.*]
Matilda?
MATTY: Yes Dad?
[DAD *splashes her.*]
MUM: Binh?
BINH: Yes?
[MUM *splashes her.*]
Ah. Charlie!
DAD: What?
BINH:
Charlie over the water ...
MUM: Aw yeah.
DAD: ⎱ [together]
MUM: ⎰
Charlie over the sea ...
ALL: Charlie broke a teapot
And blamed it onto me.
MUM: Ben!
BINH: Uh?
MATTY: It's his go.

MUM: We've got to get him.

BINH: Ah, Dad. No worries.

MUM: That's right. No worries.

DAD: I'm coming.

> [*In slow motion* DAD *moves towards them along the longest line of the stage. He splashes water at them and they splash back. Music. Laughter.*]

BINH: Me! Me! Charlie. Charlie.

> [BINH *moves to one end of the stage and stands, excited. In very, very slow motion the three move towards her gently splashing. She slowly covers her face delightedly as the water hits her. Between her fingers her smiling face is visible. In this moment* BINH *feels she has been accepted as an Australian. They all freeze. The* SINGER *comes forward.*]

SINGER: Well, that's 'The Ballad of Matilda Bell' so far. She's found one friend in the city and I expect in time there'll be plenty more. Who knows?

> [*The freeze breaks.*]

Well, thank you very much for coming. If you've enjoyed it half as much as we have, then we've enjoyed it twice as much as you have. See ya.

OTHERS: See ya.

THE END

THE SMALL POPPIES

The Small Poppies was first performed by Magpie Theatre at Theatre 62, Adelaide, on 1 March, 1986 with the following cast:

CLINT/JOHNNIE FOLEY/RONNIE FOLEY/ THIRD JOKER	Stephen Rae
LEP/THEO'S MUM/ CHI	Evdokia Katahanas
THEO/MR BRENNAN	Brian Parker
CLINT'S MUM/ CAMBODIAN/ THUAN/MARIA/ SECOND JOKER	Louise Blackwell
THEO'S DAD/SHANE MILLER /AUSTRALIAN EMBASSY MAN /HOSTEL MAN /THIRD JOKER	Richard Margetson
MRS WALSH/NOI	Melanie Salomon

Directed by Geoffrey Rush
Designed by Colin Mitchell
Lighting by John Comeadow
Music composed by Moya Henderson
Music Recorded by the Australian String Quartet

CHARACTERS
CLINT, five years old
LEP, five years old
THEO, five years old
MARIA, five years old
CHI, five years old
THUAN, five years old
SHANE MILLER, five years old
JOHNNIE FOLEY, five years old
RONNIE FOLEY, his twin brother
CLINT'S MUM, divorced
THEO'S DAD, Greek
THEO'S MUM, his wife, also Greek
NOI, LEP's older sister
MRS WALSH, the teacher
MR BRENNAN, the head teacher
AUSTRALIAN EMBASSY MAN, in Thailand
CAMBODIAN interpreter
HOSTEL MAN, a Cambodian in Adleaide
FIRST JOKER
SECOND JOKER
THIRD JOKER

Various voices off including singers, children, a Thai Airlines captain, a radio announcer, an Airport public address, a race caller

SETTING
The audience sits on three sides of the acting area. Surrounding the back of the stage and down two sides of the audience is an extensive mural of children's drawings. There are buildings, trees, some houses, school graffiti, people, clouds, sky, grass etcetera and some helicopters firing guns. At the upstage end there is a diorama of several later scenes, which is initially concealed by folding doors, blending into the general sweep of the painting.

On this area we see drawings by CLINT, LEP, THEO and MRS WALSH. Two of the houses in the mural have practical shuttered windows. There is a shutter device in one of the clouds and a tree. In one corner is a toy box with shelves.

Above: Louise Blackwell as Maria, Stephen Rae as Clint.
Below: Stephen Rae, Evdokia Katahanas as Lep, Brian Parker
as Theo. Magpie Theatre production. Photos: David Wilson.

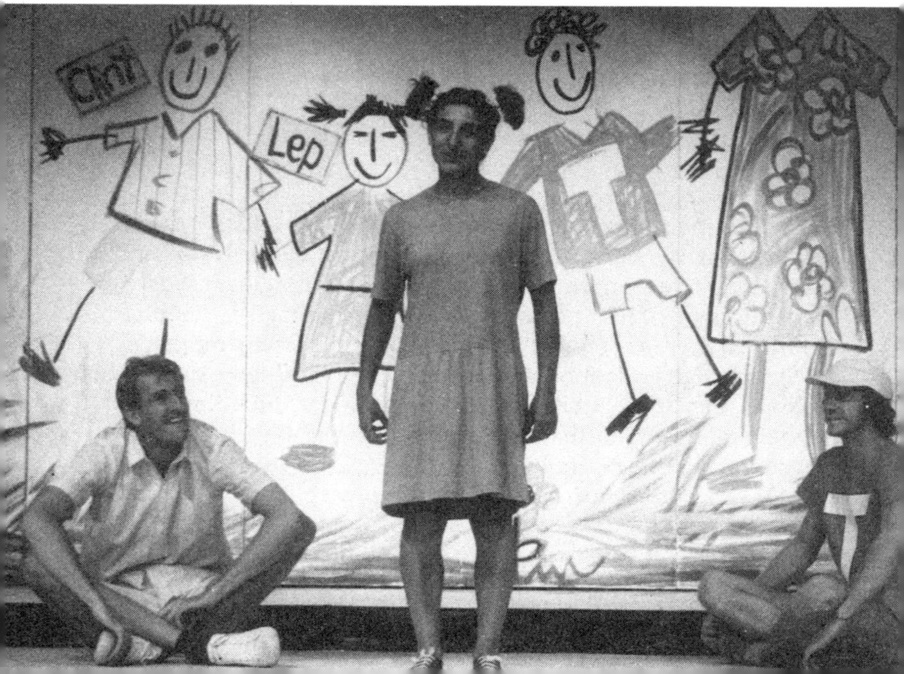

ACT ONE

As the audience arrives, young children sing their favourite songs in voice over. The lights go down. A music intro plays and the lights come up on CLINT, LEP, THEO *and* MRS WALSH *in front of the upstage doors. They are dressed like the figures in the painting.* CLINT, LEP *and* THEO *form a triangle.* MRS WALSH *watches from one side. The children do very well orchestrated hand movements to their song. It is clearly a well rehearsed routine.*

CHILDREN: [*singing*]
>A sailor went to I, I, I
>To see what he could I, I, I,
>But all that he could I,I,I
>Was the bottom of the deep blue I, I, I.

[*They laugh and go into a four-second break dance move which brings them round one place in the triangle. They freeze. Two of the shutters crash open.*]

FIRST JOKER: What did the big chimney say to the little chimney? 'You're too young to smoke.'

SECOND JOKER: [*trying to think of a joke*] Um ... um ...

FIRST JOKER: What do you call Batman and Robin when they get squashed? 'Flatman' and 'Ribbon'.

SECOND JOKER: Um ... um ...

FIRST JOKER: What did the old witch say to the twin witches? 'Which witch is which?'

[*The shutters slam shut and the threesome unfreeze and sing.*]

CHILDREN:
>A sailor went to love, love, love
>To see what he could love, love, love,
>But all that he could love, love, love
>Was the bottom of the deep blue love, love,
>>love.

[*They go into a different short break dance which brings them to new positions. They freeze. The shutters swing open.*]

FIRST JOKER: A, B, C, D, E, F, G, H, I, J, K, L, M, N, O ... Q, R, S, T, U, V, W, X, Y, Z.
[*Pause.*]
[*Irritated, prompting the* SECOND JOKER] 'What happened to the "P"?'
SECOND JOKER: I *know*. It's running down your leg.
FIRST JOKER: Nerd!
[*The shutters slam and the children unfreeze and sing.*]
CHILDREN: A sailor went to you, you, you
To see what he could you, you, you,
But all that he could you, you, you
Was the bottom of the deep blue you, you, you.

[*They go into a new short break move which brings them around one. They freeze. The shutters swing open.*]
FIRST JOKER: What do you do when your dog's in the street? Put him in a barking lot!
SECOND JOKER: [*still trying to think of a joke*] Um ... um ...
FIRST JOKER: What do you get when you -
SECOND JOKER: [*interrupting*] Knock, knock.
FIRST JOKER: Who's there?
SECOND JOKER: Pizza.
FIRST JOKER: Pizza who?
SECOND JOKER: Pizza Hut!
[*Pause.*]
FIRST JOKER: That's a good one.
[*The shutters close and the children unfreeze and sing.*]
CHILDREN: A sailor went to I love you
To see what he could I love you,
But all that he could I love you
Was the bottom of the deep blue I love you.

[*Music, and they go into a slightly more extravagant break dance. At the end of the break move, all three finish on the ground.* CLINT *rises nervously. As each child introduces themselves, they attach their name on a printed cloth applique to the drawing.* MRS WALSH *helps with the distribution. Throughout the introductions,* THEO *bounces on the floor.*]
CLINT: I did the writing for this story, did ya know? My name is Clint. Mrs Walsh's class. She helped us. My birthday is the twenty-fourth of September, nineteen eighty. My

best friend is Theo and Lep and we're getting a dog at home. And we're getting a new daddy called Eddie to live with us, did ya know?

[LEP *rises nervously*.]

LEP: My name is Lep. My best friend is Theo and Clint. I was born in Cambodia or Thailand. I don't know my real birthday but a Aussie man in Thailand present me birthday of twenty-six of January ... because Australia day. I know I was born in the Year of the Monkey and I did the drawings in this story except for the kangaroos.

[THEO *rises nervously. He is hyperactive*.]

THEO: I did the kangaroos. My name is Theo.

[*He puts his name on the drawing upside down.* MRS WALSH *corrects it for him*.]

Best friends: Clint and Lep and ...

[*Pause*.]

Brett.

[CLINT *and* LEP *look at each other, hurt*. THEO *goes on*.]

Best footy: Sturt. Best star: Cindy Lauper. Best Grand Prix: Ayrton Senna. My dad's got a Mizobushi Colt 'cause he works there and um ... when I grow up I'm ... I'm going to be Ayrton Senna. Brmmm-mmm-mmm. And um ... I'm going to have a kangaroo called 'Rocky'!

[*The group attaches two more words to the painting: 'Our Story'. They face the audience and link arms strongly so they are in line*.]

CHILDREN: Our story!

CLINT: [*moving back to the shutters*] Once.

LEP: [*moving back to the shutters*] Upon.

THEO: [*moving back*] A.

[*The jokers burst through the shutters*.]

FIRST JOKER:
SECOND JOKER: } [together] Time.

CLINT: There.

LEP: Was.

THEO: A.

FIRST JOKER:
SECOND JOKER: } [*together*] Certain.

[*The jokers disappear*.]

CHILDREN: ⎫
FIRST JOKER: ⎬ [*together*] Big, big.
SECOND JOKER: ⎭
MRS WALSH: Galaxy.
> [*Music. They move closer to* MRS WALSH, *who hands out a
> variety of large, two-dimensional props the children have
> made: stars, a comet, moon, sun, a kangaroo. They create
> a celestial pageant. As she talks, the children gather other
> appropriate props.*]

And in that galaxy there was a big planet.
> [*The Earth moves central as the others retreat.* CLINT *exits.*]

And on that planet was a certain country.
> [LEP *points with a large arrow to a slightly indistinct
> Australia. The Earth retreats as a large cut-out of Australia
> marches forward.* LEP *turns the arrow over and points to
> the big red dot for Adelaide. The arrow says 'Us'. There
> is a kangaroo on it.*]

And in that country was a city where someone was having
a very special day.
> [CLINT'S MUM *sings 'Happy Birthday' as* LEP *and* THEO
> *open the doors to reveal a picture of her and* CLINT *in their
> house.* THEO *drives off. There are holes for the heads and
> arms of the characters. 'I am five today' is written on the
> house or garden. There is a kangaroo also.* CLINT *is
> depicted at the character's real height so that his head is
> near the bottom of the picture and his* MUM'*s is near the
> top.* LEP *quickly hands her a small, brightly coloured
> present to complete the scene and runs off with the others.
> There is a label on it which says 'Happy birthday, son.'*]

CLINT'S MUM: [*singing*]
> Happy Birthday to you,
> Happy Birthday to you,
> Happy Birthday dear Clint,
> Happy Birthday to you.

Close your eyes, Clint.
CLINT: [*closing them*] Aw, what is it, Mum? Is it from real
Dad?
CLINT'S MUM: No, it bloody isn't. That bastard hasn't sent
anything this year. It's from me.
CLINT: Aw.

CLINT'S MUM: Now it's not your big prezzie. You're getting that at your party this arvo.

CLINT: Aw, what is it, Mum? A Craig McDermott cricket set?

CLINT'S MUM: No.

[CLINT *takes the present and shakes it, then feels it. Enter the bouncing* THEO *followed by* THEO'S MUM *and* THEO'S DAD. *They are real, not part of the picture.* THEO'S DAD *carries the swimming gear.* THEO'S MUM *is in bathers, a beach coat and Doctor Scholl sandals.*]

THEO'S DAD: *Ella mitera theloume na tou thousoume mathima ya kolimvi ke na kopsoume ta malya doo.* [*'Come on, Mother. We're got to give him a swimming lesson and a haircut.'*] Eh, Theo, nice short hair so you no look like bodzis.

CLINT'S MUM: [*to* CLINT] Look, Clint, that boy's going to big school the same day as you, next month.

CLINT: Yuk!

[*She clips his ear and smiles at the Greek family.*]

CLINT'S MUM: G'day.

THEO'S DAD: ⎫
THEO'S MUM: ⎭ [*together*] G'day.

THEO'S DAD: Say 'G'day', Theo.

THEO: [*reluctantly*] G'day.

CLINT'S MUM: Swimming centre again?

THEO'S DAD: My Theo he want swim good before big school. I teach.

[THEO *bounces and punches the air waiting to go.*]

THEO'S MUM: *Theo, stamata na choropithas.* [*Theo, stop bouncing!*]

THEO'S DAD: [*to* CLINT'S MUM] Big school, eh?

[*With a smile the Greek family departs with* THEO *bouncing.*]

CLINT'S MUM: Maybe that boy hasn't got someone to look out for him at big school like Maria is for you. [*Changing her tone*] Go on, open your present.

[*Pause.*]

Clint?

CLINT: Um?

[*He starts to open it.*]

CLINT'S MUM: Clint ... um ... that was Eddie on the phone before.

[*Pause.*]
He's like to come over this afternoon to see me.
[*Pause.*]
And you.
[*Pause.*]
Can I ask him to your birthday party?
CLINT: You said I could just ask Maria, remember?
CLINT'S MUM: I know.
CLINT: You *said.*
CLINT'S MUM: I *know* I *said*, Clint.
[*Pause.*]
Eddie said he'd take you to the cricket tomorrow. It's
Queensland. [*Enticingly*] Craig McDermott.
CLINT: I don't want to go to the cricket. Is he staying the
night?
CLINT'S MUM: He's got a name, Clint!
CLINT: Is he?
CLINT'S MUM: It's *'Eddie'.* I don't know. Not if you're like
you were last Saturday night, he won't.
[CLINT *smirks surreptitiously. He takes the last wrapping
off the present and looks at it without excitement.*]
[*Worried*] It's the transformer you wanted.
CLINT: [*dealing with an absolute incompetent*] Mum, I've got
an Autobot Jumpstarter. I said 'the Air Guardian'.
CLINT'S MUM: [*resignedly*] Alright, we'll go down the shop
and change it.
CLINT: [*wounded*] It's alright, Mum.
CLINT'S MUM: Aw no! Come and get your laces tied.
[*The diorama starts to move.*]
CLINT: Why?
CLINT'S MUM: Because you're not going to whinge at me all
day like you was a big sook. We're going down to that
shop and get you one of those Space Guardians. Come on!
[CLINT'S MUM *disappears.*]
CLINT: *Air* Guardians!
[CLINT *disappears to a gloomy musical phrase of 'Happy
Birthday to You'.*]
MRS WALSH: Theo at the pool.
[*She exits. The sounds of* THEO *drowning accompany the
entrance of a diorama of a swimming pool with* THEO'S DAD

in bathers holding THEO *in the water. There are holes for the characters' faces and arms. There appears to be a kangaroo in the pool.* THEO'S MUM *enters and sets up a cut-out of a towel on the stage.*]

THEO: [*fighting for air*] Glug. Glug. Glug.

THEO'S MUM: *Christos, katabini nero.* ['*Christos, he's breathing water!*']

THEO'S DAD: Theo, I got you. *Mitera, xero ti kano.* ['*Mama, I know what I'm doing.*'] Theo, head up. Up!

THEO: [*spluttering*] Dad. Why can't I float? They're going to laugh at me at big school.

THEO'S MUM: *Theo, tha isse entaxi.* ['*Theo, you'll be alright.*']

THEO'S DAD: Theo, no worries. We got one month to big school. I teach you swim so good you school champion cup butterfly. Year Two Thousand, you swim Olympic Game for Australia.

THEO'S MUM: *O Theos then kolimvi ya tin Afstralia.* ['*Theo's not swimming for Australia.*']

THEO'S DAD: Okay, he swim for Greece and Australia. [*To* THEO] Okay, Theo, you take breath. I take my hand away. You swim dog.

THEO: Okay.

THEO'S DAD: Okay? I take my hand away.

[THEO'S DAD *takes his hands away.*]

THEO: Aaagh. Glug. Glug. I'm drowning.

THEO'S MUM: Chris!

THEO'S DAD: Theo! You take breath *first*. Again!

[*Music, and the image starts to move.*]

THEO'S MUM: *Etsi boo ton thithaskis tha fovate to nero.* ['*The way you're teaching him, he'll be afraid of the water.*']

[*She picks up her towel and bag. The picture continues to move as they argue.*]

THEO'S DAD: *Ego imouna a byo kalos kolimvitis sto Pirea!* ['*I was the best swimmer in Piraeus!*'] Theo. Again!

[*The picture is almost gone.*]

THEO'S MUM: *O tropos bou tou kanis tha ton bmixis.* ['*The way you're doing it, you'll drown him.*']

THEO'S DAD: Theo. Again.

CLINT: [*off*] Maria!

THEO'S MUM: [*to* THEO'S DAD] *Ine mikros fovate to nero.* [*'The child is small. He's scared of the water.'*]

   [THEO'S MUM'*s storms off.*]

CLINT: [*off*] Maria!

   [MRS WALSH *enters with several free-standing poppies. She places them.*]

MRS WALSH: Meanwhile, in Clint's garden.

   [*She exits as* CLINT *runs on with a big, colourfully wrapped birthday present. He wears a party hat.*]

CLINT: Maria! Maria!

   [*The music ends. A picture of* CLINT'*s garden comes on, this time without holes for the characters. There are lots of poppies, a tree, a flower and a kangaroo.* CLINT *is followed by his make-believe dog.*]

Maria? Where is she, Digger? Sit! Maria, I want to show you this. Maria?

   [*And he goes wandering off to find her.*]

Come on, Digger. Good boy.

   [CLINT *exits.*]

MARIA: [*off*] Clint!

   [MARIA *enters, also in a party hat.* MRS WALSH *enters behind.*]

MRS WALSH: Clint's best friend.

   [*She drifts away.*]

MARIA:

      I'm a pretty little Dutch girl,
      As pretty as can be.

Clint!

      And all the boys in the football team
      Are crazy over me.

Clint!

      My boyfriend's name is Tony,
      He comes from Macaroni
      With his two black eyes and a button nose
      And that is how my story goes.

Clint!

   [CLINT *returns with his unopened package and watches.* MARIA *doesn't see him.*]

   [*With mimed actions*]

I L, O, V, E, love you.
I L, O, V, E, love you.
I K, I, S, S, kiss you.
So I jumped in the lake and swallowed a snake
And I gave myself a bellyache.

Clint!

CLINT: [*showing her the package*] Maria, look!

MARIA: Your mum and that man want you in for gelati.

CLINT: I'm not going in there. They're kissin'. Yuk.

MARIA: Where?

CLINT: In the kitchen. He's going like this.

[*He puts his hands inside* MARIA's *blouse.*]

MARIA: Yuk!

CLINT: Yeah. Yuk! And this.

[*He kisses* MARIA *wetly behind the ear.*]

MARIA: Uuurgh.

[CLINT *opens the parcel.*]

Good my mum and dad don't do that.

CLINT: He's not my dad. You're lucky.

[CLINT *reveals a new school bag.*]

Awww. Same as yours!

[*He gets down on his knees and opens the bag's fasteners.*
MARIA *is not as enthusiastic. She's been at school three
months.*]

MARIA: Yeah.

CLINT: Get yours!

MARIA: No.

CLINT: Awww. Let's play schools.

[*He takes out the brand new brightly coloured sandwich
container and bottle.*]

MARIA: No.

CLINT: I'm getting vegemite and banana sangers. And Milo.
Aw, and an Ovaltine Muesli Bar.

MARIA: Is he staying the night, that Eddie?

CLINT: Every Saturday now.

MARIA: Where does he sleep?

CLINT: In my mum's bed. They lock the door! I can't go in
there.

[MARIA *shakes her head at this adult perfidy.*]

CLINT'S MUM: [*off*] Clint! Maria! Gelati.   On the table!
[*Pleasantly*] Eddie! Don't!
[*The kids shake their heads at this behaviour. It's a sad
state of affairs.*]
CLINT: Where do you sit in Mrs Walsh's class? I'm going to
sit at your table dead set.
MARIA: Next to her.
CLINT: [*apprehensively*] Is Shane Miller on that table?
MARIA: Denissa, Brett, Dallas, Soraya, me and Shane Miller.
[MARIA *makes a gesture indicating exactly what she does
to deal with Shane Miller.* CLINT *smiles. He'll be protected.*]
CLINT: Aw, kookaburras.
MARIA: You're not going to be a kookaburra.   Newies are
wombats.
CLINT: I want to be a kookaburra with you!
MARIA: [*mimicking* MRS WALSH] You're a very naughty boy,
Clint. You're a wombat. [*Indicating his bag*] And we do
not bring our bags into class except for show and tell. We
hang them in the corridor.
CLINT: Yes, Mrs Walsh.
MARIA: And did I say bring a pretend dog into my classroom?
CLINT: No, Mrs Walsh. Out, Digger! Right out. Wait for me
in the sand pit.
[*They watch the make-believe Digger go.*]
MARIA: You're not at kindy now, Clint. Dallas! Stop poking
Maria. Big school is *work*, Clint. Big school is *learning*.
Shane, I'm not telling you again.
[*She bashes Shane.*]
Right, all you newies. Wombats. Make yourself as tall as
a house.
[CLINT *gladly does so.*]
Make yourself as small as a mouse. Denissa, I'm not talking
to you again.   Nor Fung Me.   Ohhh, we've got some
chatterboxes here today.
CLINT'S MUM: [*off*] Maria! Clint!
MARIA: Show and tell. I'm going to ask the person with the
happiest face.
[CLINT'*s face is a fixed, steely grin.* MARIA *looks around
at other imagined faces.* THEO *enters with a pullover round*

his head. He is not bouncing. CLINT'*s grin is immediately wiped off. Pause.*]

THEO: [*tearfully*] Can I play with youse?

MARIA: [*to* CLINT, *sotto voce*] Yuk.

CLINT: [*sotto voce*] He's had a haircut for big school. Look.

MARIA: He he he.

[CLINT *rises and goes over to* THEO.]

CLINT: You can play ...

[*And whips the pullover off, showing a shorn* THEO] Baldies.

[THEO *tears the pullover back and wraps it round his head.* CLINT *laughs and goes back to* MARIA.]

THEO: Yus dickheads. What yus playing?

MARIA: Haircuts.

[*She bursts into laughter.*]

CLINT: [*laughing*] Yeah. Haircuts.

THEO: [*holding out lollies*] Be yus' best friend.

[CLINT *moves to take a lolly.* MARIA *stops him.*]

MARIA: We're having *gelati*.

CLINT: Yeah. And I've got a best friend.

MARIA: Rack off, Baldy.

CLINT: Yeah. Rack off.

[THEO *slowly, painfully, with great sadness, racks off.* CLINT *and* MARIA *poke and nudge each other with great delight.*]

CLINT'S MUM: [*off*] Clint. Maria. I'm throwing this strawberry and banana gelati into the rubbish.

MARIA: }
CLINT: } [*together*] Nooo.

[*And they run inside. Music plays. Enter the Australian* EMBASSY MAN. *As he speaks, the lights dim.*]

EMBASSY MAN: [*to the audience*] Now the story has to go a very very long way from Australia: to the border of two countries called Cambodia and Thailand. It is night, in a camp for refugees of the war in Cambodia. Two young Cambodian girls are asleep among thousands of people.

[*The outline of two figures lying on the ground under blankets can be made out in the centre of the stage. The mural goes dark and becomes a jungle at night. The music continues. Far away is the sound of gunfire, then silence. Off, a car roars to a halt. Doors open and slam. Footsteps.*

*The beams of two electric torches come towards the blankets.
The torches shine down on the two girls:* LEP *and* NOI. *The
torch light shines on on one of the men: the* EMBASSY MAN.
He holds papers.]

[*Whispering, reading*] I have Australian passports for a
mother and two girls called 'Noi' and 'Lep'. Let's see if
this is the kids?

[*The* CAMBODIAN INTERPRETER *shines his torch on the two
girls and shakes the blanket. They wake up in fright and
clutch each other.*]

[*To the girls*] It's alright. It's alright. [*To the* CAMBODIAN]
Ask them.

[*He shines his torch on the* CAMBODIAN, *who shines the
other on the two girls. The* CAMBODIAN *takes the papers
and shows them to the two girls.*]

CAMBODIAN: Noi?

[NOI *looks at her sister and then slowly points to herself.*]
Lep?

[LEP *nods.*]

[*To the* EMBASSY MAN] This is them. [*To the girls*] *Eng
kheunh lok nis te? Kort mok pi protes Australie.* [*'You see
this man here? From Australia.'*]

[*He points the torch at the* EMBASSY MAN, *who shows them
a small Australian flag, then two passports.*]

EMBASSY MAN: Passports. Australian.

CAMBODIAN: [*to the girls*] *Kort tha; Australie neung yok eng.
Tov rous nov ti nuos.* [*'This man says Australia will take
you. You can live there.' To the* EMBASSY MAN] I tell them
Australia their home now.

EMBASSY MAN: Why don't they say anything?

CAMBODIAN: They live in bad camp all their lives, sir. They
don't have hope.

EMBASSY MAN: Have they learnt any English in this place?

CAMBODIAN: [*to the girls*] *Anglais?* [*'English?'*]

NOI: [*slowly, with a heavy accent*] Sit. Stand. Go. Come.
Bloody bastard.

EMBASSY MAN: Jeez.

CAMBODIAN: I show them air tickets to Australia. [*To the
girls*] *Samboit yun hors pi san loek nis. Neung dok eng*

chenh. *Pi pror tes Thai. Toe eng chang tou te?* ['*Two tickets to take you from Thailand. You want?*']

[*He holds out the tickets.* NOI *ignores the tickets and pats the Australian's pockets for food. The* EMBASSY MAN *takes food from his other pocket and gives it to both.*]

NOI: [*indicating the food*] Australia?

EMBASSY MAN: [*giving more food to both*] Australia, yes. Yes, we have food in Australia.

LEP: Australia.

EMBASSY MAN: [*gesturing to the papers*] Where's their mother?

CAMBODIAN: [*to the girls*] *Makyom?* ['*Mother?*']

[*Gunfire sounds far off.* NOI *gestures to it in answer to his question. Their mother is dead. The Australian and the* CAMBODIAN *look at each other.*]

[*To the girls*] *Toe eng chane tou rous tov protes Australie te?* ['*You want to live in Australia?*']

[LEP *looks at* NOI. NOI *nods and puts her hand out for the flag. The* EMBASSY MAN *gives it.*]

EMBASSY MAN: [*to the* CAMBODIAN] Tell them they're flying very soon. From Bangkok.

CAMBODIAN: [*rising to leave*] *Eng neung chark chenh tou protes Australie. Knong peil chhab chhab his noey.* ['*You'll be leaving soon for Australia.*']

[*They are about to depart when* LEP, *illuminated by the Australian's torch, reaches for the other. The* EMBASSY MAN *nods and the* CAMBODIAN *gives the torch to* LEP. *The two leave. The girls are left alone to inspect their flag in the torchlight.* LEP *takes the flag and gives it a little wave. They start to laugh. She points to the flag.*]

LEP: Australia.

[NOI *puts the blanket over* LEP *and, with one last look at the flag, turns the torch off as the music rises. Darkness.*]

CHILDREN'S VOICES: [*very softly*]

> Post lady, post lady,
> Did you bring a letter?
> Post lady, post lady,
> Two would suit me better.
> I can hardly wait to see
> What is in your bag for me.

[*The lights come slowly up to reveal* MR BRENNAN *and a pop-out desk.* MR BRENNAN *completes the picture by pulling out a sliding panel which says 'Head Teacher' in English, Greek, Italian and Vietnamese. Humming to himself, he takes a large computer instruction book or envelope from the shelves.*]

MR BRENNAN: [*to himself, singing*] '...Blue, blue, blue suede ...' [*Reading*] One twenty-eight K, built in disc drive ...
[*He pops up a computer from his desk.*]
The new school computer. At last ... Hmmm ... [*Singing*] 'Shoes, you can do anything, but don't step ...' [*To his secretary, off*] Cathy, can you give me ten minutes so I can master this machine?
[*He sits at the computer. Still looking at the book he starts pressing keys.*]
'Boot in the disk.' [*Pressing more keys, singing*] 'You can knock me down, step on my ...'

CATHY: [*off*] Mr Brennan, Mr Papadopoulous has come in to have a word with you.

MR BRENNAN: Who?

CATHY: [*off*] About Theo.

MR BRENNAN: Send him in, please. [*To the machine*] Boy. [*Pressing keys*] B, O, Y.
[*He smiles and waves to the screen.* THEO'S DAD *enters, watches and then* ...]
Mr Papadopoulous, g'day. [*Indicating the other chair*] Please.
[*He turns to the window.* THEO'S DAD *looks at the computer.*]
Troy, don't swing on that drainpipe, mate. It took your dad all weekend to mend it.

THEO'S DAD: Space Invade?

MR BRENNAN: No. Reading Programme. If I could afford one for each class, Mr Papadopoulous, we could improve the reading in this school twenty percent. Show you? [*Shouting to* CATHY, *off*] Cathy, any chance of a cup of coffee for Mr Papadopoulous please? [*To* THEO'S DAD] Milk? Sugar?

THEO'S DAD: No.

MR BRENNAN: [*shouting to* CATHY, *off*] No milk, no sugar.

THEO'S DAD: No. No coffee. Listen, Mr Brennan. I think I change my mind about Theo come here your school. Okay? Sorry. I think I take him other one.

MR BRENNAN: Mr Papadopoulous, you choose the school. If you've found a school where Theo's going to be happy, I'm happy. [*Shouting out the window*] Tracy!

[*He shakes his head.*]

Good girl. [*To* THEO'S DAD] See, when I press this, a three-letter word comes up here.

THEO'S DAD: 'Cat'.

MR BRENNAN: Okay. As soon as it comes up, a picture of a little boy in a hot air balloon starts coming down the screen and I've got to tap out - [*Typing*] 'C, A, T' before he gets to the bottom.

[*Pause.*]

Got him!

THEO'S DAD: Hey, the balloon and boy, they go up fly.

MR BRENNAN: Right, and he waves at you, see? That's a reward for the kids when they spell it right.

THEO'S DAD: [*pleased*] Hey! Good.

MR BRENNAN: [*moving aside*] Have a go, Mr Papadopoulous.

THEO'S DAD: [*moving to* MR BRENNAN'*s seat*] Hey no. I no typewrite.

MR BRENNAN: Neither can most of my preps. Go!

[*And he presses the keys.*]

THEO'S DAD: 'Dog'. Oh, no. Where is D? I make car engine, I don't ... Ah. D. Where is O? O, O, O, O, O! [*Finding it*] O!

MR BRENNAN: 'Bout three seconds!

THEO'S DAD: G? Where is G? G. G. G. G. G. Oh, no. I lose. The little boy drown.

MR BRENNAN: No worries. Try again.

[MARIA *enters.*]

Hello, Maria. Is young Clint looking forward to starting school with us next week?

MARIA: Yes Mr Brennan. Mr Brennan ...

MR BRENNAN: [*pressing a key for* THEO'S DAD] It's not dibberdobbing again is it?

THEO'S DAD: Jam! J, J, J, J ...

MARIA: Mr Brennan, there's love writing on the toilet windows.

THEO'S DAD: A, A, A, A, A, A, A ...

MR BRENNAN: Love writing?

THEO'S DAD: M, M, M, M, M, M, M ...

MARIA: 'Fe uu ce kissing ke.'

THEO'S DAD: [*victoriously*] Hey!

MARIA: I seen one of the Foley twins do it.

THEO'S DAD: [*pointing at the TV screen*] The little boy. He fly!

> [THEO'S DAD *smiles and waves at the little boy on the screen.*]

MR BRENNAN: Ask Mr Baxter to get out the Jiff, Maria, okay? And rub it off. Which of those twins was it? Was it Johnnie or Ronnie?

> [MARIA *makes a helpless gesture.*]

Tell both twins to come here. Now.

MARIA: [*leaving*] Yes, Mr Brennan.

THEO'S DAD: [*indicating the screen*] Jam!

MR BRENNAN: Excellent. So which school for Theo, Mr Papadopoulous, do you think? Riverside? Saint Theresa?

> [THEO'S DAD *indicates he is still unsure.*]

Riverside's a good school.

THEO'S DAD: Riverside good but far away.

MR BRENNAN: Saint Theresa is good.

THEO'S DAD: Good, but Catholic school.

MR BRENNAN: Hmmm.

THEO'S DAD: Your school also good, but ...

MR BRENNAN: Hmmm?

THEO'S DAD: All these Vietnamese. The hostel near. Not your fault.

MR BRENNAN: Oh, don't worry. I like 'em. How many do you think we've got, Mr Papadopoulous?

> [THEO'S DAD *takes in nearly the whole school with a gesture.*]

Only eight. Four Cambodians, three Czechs, four Chileans, a Bulgar. We've got Italians, Yugoslavs, but mostly good old Irish and Greek. Oh, and one Pom. Me.

> [*There is a knock at the door.*]

[*Shouting*] Come! [*To* THEO'S DAD] Excuse me. [*Offering the computer book*] Here.

[*A Foley twin enters.*]
Johnnie?
RONNIE: No, Mr Brennan. Ronnie.
MR BRENNAN: Ronnie. Love writing?
RONNIE: Eh?
MR BRENNAN: Toilet windows?
RONNIE: Me, Mr Brennan? No, Mr Brennan. I been playing footy. Must be my brother.
MR BRENNAN: Johnnie?
RONNIE: Yes, Mr Brennan.
MR BRENNAN: Send *him* in.
> [RONNIE *goes.*]
[*To* THEO'S DAD] Terrific actors, Mr Papadopoulous, these Foley twins. They're better than Mel Gibson.
> [*A knock and a Foley twin stands at the door: the same actor in the same clothes.*]
Isn't he there?
JOHNNIE: Who, Mr Brennan?
MR BRENNAN: Johnnie.
JOHNNIE: *I'm* Johnnie, Mr Brennan.
MR BRENNAN: Ah. Now, Johnnie, love wr- ... Why can't you twins wear different clothes to school? Stupid question. Why make it easy for the teachers? Johnnie. Love writing?
JOHNNIE: Eh?
MR BRENNAN: On the toilet windows. Not you?
JOHNNIE: No, Mr Brennan.
MR BRENNAN: Playing footy at the time?
JOHNNIE: No, Mr Brennan.
> [*A beat.*]
Basketball
MR BRENNAN: Haven't got time now. After school here. Enjoy your weekend?
JOHNNIE: Yes Mr Brennan.
MR BRENNAN: Catch anything?
JOHNNIE: European carp, Mr Brennan.
> [*He indicates a length of about five feet.*]
MR BRENNAN: I believe you, Johnnie.
> [JOHNNIE *goes.*]

Mr Papadopoulous, I'm just going to pop along to Mrs Walsh's class. That's where we were going to put Theo. Have you got a minute?

THEO'S DAD: Sure, but -

MR BRENNAN: [*interrupting, shouting off*] Cathy, back in a quarter of an hour. [*Shouting at the window*] Brett! [*To* THEO'S DAD] After you.

  [*Blackout.*]

CHILDREN'S VOICES:

> I went to a Chinese restaurant
> To buy a loaf of bread bread bread,
> But when I asked the name of this,
> This is what he said said said:

> My name is
> Errolai Errolai
> Chickolai Chickolai
> Oooly Oooly
> Rum Pum Pum
> Wally Wally Whiskas
> Chinese Kiskas.
> Do me a favour,
> Drop dead. Smarty head.

  [*They laugh and the lights go up on* MRS WALSH *and a class of* MARIA *and* CHI. *A section of blackboard has been folded out near the shelves.* MR BRENNAN *and* THEO'S DAD *enter.*]

MRS WALSH: Now, children, we've got a visitor. Can we say 'Good morning' to Mr Papadopoulous.

CHILDREN: [*droning*] Good morning, Mr Pap ...

MRS WALSH: Mr Pap-a-dop-o-lous.

CHILDREN: Good morning Mr Papad ...

THEO'S DAD: No worries. Name 'Chrees'.

CHILDREN: Good morning, Mr Chrees.

MRS WALSH: And perhaps Mr Papadopoulous will be able to help us with what we're doing this morning.

THEO'S DAD: [*bemused, waving his hands*] No. No teacher.

MRS WALSH: Chi?

THEO'S DAD: [*to* MR BRENNAN, *whispering*] Vietnamese?

  [MR BRENNAN *nods.* THEO'S DAD *makes a gesture to express his sympathy for* MR BRENNAN, *having so many of them in*

*the class. The teacher opens a book with a face on it and
a Greek question written above it.*]

MRS WALSH: [*pointing to the face, with a passable accent*] Ki.
Ti ine?' ['*Chi. What is it?*']

CHI: [*pointing at her own face*] Afta ine to prosobo moo. ['*This
is my face.*']

[THEO'S DAD *turns, jaw open.*]

THEO'S DAD: Eh?

MRS WALSH: [*pointing at the picture*] Ki, ti ine? ['*Chi, what
is this?*']

CHI: [*pointing*] Afta ine ta hilli moo. ['*This is my lips.*']

THEO'S DAD: [*whispering to* MR BRENNAN] Vietnamese, she
speak Greek?

MRS WALSH: Was that alright, Mr Papadopoulous?

THEO'S DAD: Hm! Sorry. I ...

[CHI *turns round to look at* THEO'S DAD.]

MRS WALSH: I'm not Greek, so ...

THEO'S DAD: [*to* CHI, *perfectly*] Afta ine to prosobo moo. Afta
ine ta hilli moo. ['*This is my face. This is my lips.*']

CHI: *Afta ine to prosobo moo. Afta ine ta hilli moo.*

THEO'S DAD: [*to* MRS WALSH] 'S good. [*To* CHI] Afta ine to
prosobo moo, afta ine ta hilli moo.

CHI: [*in slightly better Greek*] Afta ine to prosobo moo. Afta
ine ta hilli moo.

MRS WALSH: [*to* THEO'S DAD] Good?

THEO'S DAD: Hey, this girl from Athens?

[CHI *smiles, confused.*]

MRS WALSH: Athens is the biggest city in Greece, Chi. Like
Saigon, eh? Very famous.

CHI: Athens.

[CHI *nods respectfully to* THEO'S DAD.]

THEO'S DAD: Athens. Greece!

[THEO'S DAD *makes a proud gesture, then touches* CHI's
head. He nods at MR BRENNAN. *This is education. The
lights fade to blackout.*]

CHILDREN'S VOICES: [*singing*]
     Kefali, omi, yonnatta, thaktila,
     Kefali, omi, yonnatta, thaktila,
     Matya, miti, stoma, ke ftya,
     Kefali, omi yonnatta, thaktila.

> ['*Head, shoulders, knees, toes,*
> *Head, shoulders, knees, toes,*
> *Eyes, nose, mouth and ears,*
> *Head, shoulders, knees, toes.*']

VOICE: *Ela ksana!* ['*Once again!*']
CHILDREN'S VOICES: [*singing*]
> *Kefali, omi, yonnatta, thaktila,*
> *Kefali, omi, yonnatta, thaktila,*
> *Matya, miti, stoma, ke ftya,*
> *Kefali, omi yonnatta, thaktila.*

[*The lights fade up on the interior of a Thai Airlines cabin. LEP and NOI are seated on a raised level at the side of the mural surrounded by clouds. They are asleep under a blanket that reads 'Thai Airlines'. Music accompanies the scene.*]

CAPTAIN: [*voice over*] Good morning ladies and gentlemen, this is Captain Siniatchorn once more. Thai Airlines hope you enjoyed our in-flight movie *Mad Max Three.*

[NOI *starts to wake up.*]

We are currently cruising at thirty-one thousand feet at an airspeed of six hundred and seventy miles an hour. Very shortly my cabin staff will be distributing immigration cards to all passengers. In a moment or two I hope in spite of light cloud passengers in window seats will be able to get their first view of land as we cross the coast of Western Australia. Thank you.

[NOI *shakes* LEP *awake, which takes a few seconds. The whole of the message is repeated in Thai as background to the following:* NOI *wakes* LEP *up.* LEP *is confused.* NOI *leans over her to look out the window. Eventually she points down with some excitement.*]

LEP: *Sui noo?* ['*What is that?*']
NOI: Australia.
LEP: Australia? *Dad Mad Max now de noo day?* ['*Is Mad Max down there?*']

[NOI *laughs and waves to the ground.*]

NOI: *Sus ta ee, Mad Max!* ['*Hello, Mad Max!*']
LEP: *Sus ta ee, Mad Max!*

[*The lights go down. The musical intro to* Play School *plays and the lights go up on* CLINT's *garden. He enters*] *from the house flying his school bag through the air like a plane.*]

CLINT: [*singing*]
> I'm Popeye the sailor man,
> I live in a caravan.
> I eat all the worms
> And spit out the germs,
> I'm Popeye the sailor man.

CLINT'S MUM: [*off*] Clint, you'll wear that bag out before you get to big school.

CLINT: No I won't.

CLINT'S MUM: [*off*] *Playschool*'s on.

CLINT: I'm five now! Call me when it's *Inspector Gadget*.
[*He sets his bag up as a cricket wicket and goes back for his run up with an imaginary ball.*]
Craig McDermott. Digger, you're umpy.
[CLINT *runs in and bowls.*]
[*To Digger*] Howzat!
[*He turns to the imaginary Digger behind him and kicks over his bag to indicate a broken wicket.*]
[*To Digger*] Eh?
[CLINT *puts his own finger up, then jumps in the air.*]
Ripper!
[MARIA *enters, very fed up indeed.*]
Maria, you bat. I'll bowl. Digger's umpy.
[*She shakes her head.*]
Let's play schools. I ... What's the matter?

MARIA: Dad.

CLINT: What?

MARIA: He's ...

CLINT: What?

MARIA: Factory's closing.

CLINT: Yeah?

MARIA: He's got a new job.

CLINT: Good.

MARIA: Near the port.

CLINT: He's got a car.

MARIA: He says he hasn't got the petrol money. We're getting a house over there.

CLINT: Awww. No! But he' got to bring you back to big school here.

[MARIA *shakes her head.*]

What?

[*He realises.*]

Aw, nooo. No. You ... What about me? Who am I going to school with? Shane Miller will bash me! Mum! I'll tell my mum to tell your dad.

MARIA: She won't tell him.

[*She lets go a full-blooded scream, kicks* CLINT'*s bag over, starts crying and exits.* CLINT *cries. He puts his arms around the imaginary dog.*]

CLINT: Digger! Shane Miller! Awww nooo. Maria! Nooo.

[THEO *slowly enters, bouncing. He still has the pullover wrapped round his head. He watches* CLINT *crying.* THEO *smiles.* CLINT *stops crying.* CLINT *tries to be reconciliatory. He reaches into his bag.*]

I've got ...

[THEO *watches till* CLINT *brings out the lollies, then turns and leaves as Ayrton Senna.*]

THEO: Brmmm-mmm-mmm.

[THEO *exits.*]

CLINT'S MUM: [*off*] Clint, what's all that noise?

CLINT: Mum, I don't want to go to big school.

CLINT'S MUM: [*off*] Silly. Of course you do.

CLINT: Not on my own. I don't. I don't. I don't. I don't. Digger!

[*He clasps the imaginary dog in great desperation as the lights go down. The Airport P.A. starts almost immediately.*]

AIRPORT P.A.: For people meeting passengers from Thai Airlines Flight T-Two fifty-five, this plane has landed and passengers are clearing customs.

[*The lights come up. Back-lit through the gauze that was* CLINT'*s garden is a picture of Adelaide International Airport. The tails of several stationary jets are visible: Qantas, Alitalia and Thai Airways. The frame of the diorama should create the impression of the Airport window. There is an extra kangaroo on the Qantas plane.* LEP *and* NOI *slowly enter with their hand baggage, close together and looking around, bewildered. They hold each other.*]

AIRPORT P.A.: Will those passengers transferring to flights for Mount Gambier, Alice Springs or Port Lincoln please proceed to the domestic terminal. Thank you.

[*A Cambodian man from the hostel enters. Pause. He sees the girls.*]

HOSTEL MAN: Lep? Noi?

[*They nod.*]

Som swa khom neung Australie. [*'Welcome to Australia.'*]

[*He puts his arms out. They run to him and hug a long time. Blackout.*]

CLINT: Mum?

CLINT'S MUM: Yes, Clint?

[*The lights fade up on* CLINT'*s house.* CLINT'S MUM *does her hair with a brush. She is dolled up.*]

CLINT: Your hair's different.

CLINT'S MUM: I set it.

CLINT: Why?

CLINT'S MUM: Because I'm going out. I've told you that ten times.

CLINT: Aw, no. With *him*?

CLINT'S MUM: [*calmly*] Yes.

CLINT: Aw, Mum, don't go!

CLINT'S MUM: Clint, Eddie and me are going late-night shopping to get you something nice to wear to big school. Then we're going for a pizza. Julie Ann's baby-sitting.

CLINT: Aw, no.

CLINT'S MUM: You like Julie Ann.

CLINT: I don't!

CLINT'S MUM: Clint, we're going.

CLINT: There's a pizza car. The Graziani Brothers. They bring it. It's on TV.

CLINT'S MUM: What, so you can ignore Eddie? No thanks.

CLINT: He's staying tonight, isn't he?

CLINT'S MUM: I bloody hope so, Clint. Yes.

CLINT: Why?

CLINT'S MUM: Tell you when you're sixteen.

CLINT: Mum, don't go. Read me a story.

CLINT'S MUM: Julie Ann will.

CLINT: Mum, don't go, please! Please!

CLINT'S MUM: I haven't been out for two weeks, Clint!

CLINT: Mum, I want you. Don't go out.

CLINT'S MUM: [*weakening*] Clint, I'm going, lovey. I won't be long.

CLINT: Not tonight, Mum, please. I don't know anybody at big school now. Nobody. I want you, Mum. Tell him. Please!

[*Pause.* CLINT'S MUM *is caught by her mixed feelings and totally frustrated.*]

CLINT'S MUM: Oh, Jesus Christ, get your story book.

[CLINT *races to do so. He finds it in the toy box.* CLINT'S MUM *holds herself.*]

Oh, Eddie. Eddie. Eddie.

[CLINT *returns with the story book.*]

CLINT: Mum, you're sitting on Digger! You've killed him!

CLINT'S MUM: Aw, Jesus. Sorry Digger. I thought you'd grown out of that dog.

CLINT: No. Aw, good dog. Come here, Dig.

[CLINT *sits as his* MUM *takes the book.*]

CLINT'S MUM: I'm going to be so glad when you're at school, Clint. Then maybe I can do a couple of things I want to do.

CLINT: I'm not going. Read.

CLINT'S MUM: [*slowly, determined*] Clint ... you're going. Monday morning, bright and early, you're going. Right Digger? Right.

[*She opens the book.*]

Cinderella. You listening, you two?

[CLINT *puts his arms around the invisible dog.*]

CLINT: Listen, Digger, this one's good.

CLINT'S MUM: Once upon a time ...

[*The lights fade. Music plays.*]

RADIO ANNOUNCER: Good morning to all of you out there in the city. It's a bright bright Monday morning and the temperature at six in the a.m. is a fast-rising eighteen degrees.

[*He plays a burst of Chuck Berry's 'School Days'. The lights rise, bright. The backdrop is a large sun with a smiling face.* THEO *runs through the door with his school bag already on his back and the pullover round his head.*]

THEO: No, Dad!

[THEO'S DAD *follows him, dressed in Mitsubishi overalls and carrying a camera. The music fades.*]

THEO'S DAD: Theo, for photo you take that bloody silly thing off.

THEO: No, Dad. They'll laugh at me.

THEO'S DAD: Theo, your uncle in Athens want picture of you first day at school, your cousins in Salonika same thing, your grandfather in Toronto, and me and your mother ... and we don't want you look like Ayatollah. We want see your hair.

THEO: [*taking off the pullover*] I haven't got any hair!

THEO'S DAD: You got plenty hair. Now stand in front of the Colt. I want them to see new car in the photo.

[THEO *pops up a cut-out car and stands sluggishly in front of it.*]

No. No. No. I can't see car. Okay. Now smile. Big smile.

[THEO *grimaces.*]

Okay, one more. This time inside car so they can see I got stereo. And then ...

[*He clasps* THEO.]

Big school.

[*Blackout.*]

VOICES: [*singing*]

>Good morning, good morning,
>Good morning everyone.
>The birdies sing,
>The sky is blue
>And brightly shines the sun.

[*Fade up the sounds of kids playing. The shutters fly open.*]

SECOND JOKER: What's black and white and red all over? A skunk with a nappy rash.

FIRST JOKER: What did Tarzan say when he saw the elephants coming over the hill? 'Here come the elephants.' What did Tarzan say when he saw the elephants coming over the hill with dark sunglasses? Nothing, he didn't recognise them.

SECOND JOKER: Why did the jellybean jump off the cliff?

FIRST JOKER: Because he thought he was a smartie. Knock, knock.

SECOND JOKER: Who's there?

FIRST JOKER: Nicholas.

SECOND JOKER: 'Nicholas' who?

FIRST JOKER: Knickerless girls shouldn't climb trees.

[*He laughs and slams the shutter closed.*]

SECOND JOKER: What animal needs to be oiled? Mice, because they go 'Squeak, squeak.' What did the skeleton say to the toilet? 'You won't get much out of me.' [*To the audience*] Knock, knock!

[*The audience responds. 'Who's there?'*]

Boo.

[*'"Boo" who?'*]

I'd cry too if I had a face like yours.

[*He laughs and closes his shutter. Music starts. The lights go up.* THEO *arrives with his* DAD *in Mitsubishi overalls.* THEO *has his school bag on and his hand protecting the pullover around his head. They stop and* THEO'S DAD *tries to take* THEO's *hand from his head.* THEO's *other hand goes to hold the pullover on.* THEO'S DAD *tries again.* THEO *resists it again.* THEO'S DAD *turns away, angry. He mimes the question, 'Do you want me to stay?'* THEO *shakes his head.* THEO'S DAD *turns away and* THEO *grabs his hand, then lets it go.* THEO'S DAD *indicates he will wait over at the gate.* THEO *nods. Waving,* THEO'S DAD *slowly moves away, then makes a swimming motion to* THEO. THEO *nods and his* DAD, *waving again, moves off.* THEO *clamps the pullover round his head, gives a small bounce and punch in the air to get his confidence up. He waits.* THEO *watches as* CLINT *is pulled on by his* MUM. CLINT'S MUM *tidies him up.* CLINT *takes off his bag and throws it down.* CLINT'S MUM *picks it up.* CLINT'S MUM *gestures at how nice* THEO *is being. She shows* CLINT *his lunch box and his bottle. She puts them in the bag and hands it to him. He refuses.* CLINT'S MUM *hits him behind the knees. He gives way to silent tears.* THEO *bounces, glad to see* CLINT *humiliated, then quietly interested.* CLINT'S MUM *points at her watch and makes a small move to go.* CLINT *grabs her hand. She indicates* THEO *is watching. He loosens. She tries to kiss*

him and he turns away. She moves away. CLINT *stands
with his arms out to her.* THEO *watches, bouncing.* CLINT
looks across at THEO. THEO *takes something out of his bag
and starts eating. He turns away from* CLINT. CLINT *turns
back to where his* MUM *has departed. He cries and jumps
with frustration.* THEO *turns to where his* DAD *has gone,
then turns back. Enter* NOI *and* LEP *without school bags.*
NOI *carries a plastic aircraft bag.* CLINT *and* THEO *both
turn to watch, then turn away, superior. They are not
interested.* NOI *gives* LEP *the plastic bag and then takes a
margarine container out with a Cambodian meal in it. She
opens it and shows* LEP *the food.* CLINT *and* THEO *turn:
they smell something they don't like.* NOI *straightens her
sister's hair and looks at her.* LEP *nods.* NOI *goes.* LEP
stands there holding onto her lunch. THEO *puts his hand
to his nose.* LEP *tightens her grip on the food.* THEO *bounces,
holding his nose.* CLINT *sees this and does the same. As
soon as* CLINT *does it,* THEO *stops. He eats a lolly.* CLINT
*stops and looks to where his mother has gone. His arms
go out to her again as the bell goes.* THEO *heads off.* LEP
is confused, looks around and then follows. CLINT, *still
looking back, moves slowly off. He wipes his eyes and
follows. Pause. Enter* THEO'S DAD, CLINT'S MUM *and* NOI,
waving after the children. THEO'S DAD *makes a swimming
motion and waves at* CLINT'S MUM. *She waves back, then
cries.* THEO'S DAD *passes a tissue. She takes it and wipes
her eyes. Another bell. They exit, waving,* CLINT'S MUM
crying.]

MALE TEACHER: [*off*] In lines, please. Brett!

[THEO, CLINT *and* LEP *come on. They are in a line.* THEO
and LEP *look ahead,* CLINT *looks back. The music continues.*]

[*Off*] Mr Kiernan's line is very straight. Mrs Walsh's class?
Not very straight, Stewart! Good morning, children. We're
welcoming three newies to the school today. Theo.

[THEO *gives a small wave.*]

[*Off*] Lep. Lep's here with us from Cambodia. Lep?

[LEP *follows* THEO'*s lead and gives a small move of the
hand.*]

[*Off*] And Clint. Clint?

[CLINT *gives a tiny move of the hand.*]

[*Off*] Will Mrs Walsh's class put up their hands, please? Clint, Lep and Theo, will you join Mrs Walsh's class?
> [*They do so.*]

And I know you're going to make sure that they have a lovely first day as school. Mrs Walsh's class, please.
> [THEO *bounces off. After a pause,* LEP *follows.* CLINT *remains alone, looking back.*]

[*Gently*] Clint? Clint?

CLINT: [*wailing gigantically*] *Muuummmyyy!*
> [*The lights snap to black and the music climaxes. The house lights fade up.*]

END OF ACT ONE

ACT TWO

As the audience returns it is greeted by the new diorama of
MRS WALSH's *classroom, in which* MRS WALSH *is depicted with
her class of Iranians, Khmers, Vietnamese, Italian, Greek and
Anglo-Irish children. There is also a kangaroo. The caption
is 'Mrs Walsh's Class'. Music plays as the lights fade to
blackout. Silence.*

GREG'S VOICE: Good morning Mrs Walsh.
MRS WALSH'S VOICE: Good morning, Greg.
JADE'S VOICE: Good morning Mrs Walsh.
MRS WALSH: Good morning, Jade.
SORAYA'S VOICE: Good morning Mrs Walsh.
MRS WALSH: Good morning, Soraya.
    [*The lights fade up on the shutters and they open.*]
FIRST JOKER: Why did the boy take his car to school?
SECOND JOKER: To drive the teacher up the wall. What's green
    and flies?
FIRST JOKER: Super pickle. Ten cats in a boat. One jumped
    out. How many left?
SECOND JOKER: Nine.
FIRST JOKER: No. None!
    [*The* SECOND JOKER *laughs.*]
SECOND JOKER: That's a good one.
    [*The shutters close.*]
SHANE'S VOICE: Good morning Mrs Walsh.
    [*The lights come up on the stage.* MRS WALSH *stands in
    front of* CLINT, LEP *and* THEO *who are in line. They are
    now without their school bags.*]
MRS WALSH: Good morning, Shane. [*To the rest of the class*]
    I want the Magpies and the Kookaburras to get on with their
    activity while I show the newies the school. Dillen, don't
    interrupt when I'm talking, darling. [*To the three*] Right.
    [*They take one step to the right.*]
    Now, darlings, you've seen where you're going to be for
    the next year. Next to us is Mr Kiernan's classroom. And...
    [*They take another step to the right.*]
    This is Miss Bartolomei's classroom. And ...

[*They take another step to the right.*]

This is Mr Sheahan's classroom.

[*They look into the classroom.*]

Yes. They're very big children, aren't they?

[CLINT *gives a long wail. Bouncing,* THEO *puts his hand up.*]

Yes, Theo?

THEO: Mrs Walsh, we've got a Mitsubishi Colt.

MRS WALSH: Very good, Theo. We start off every morning with an activity.

[*Over the following she gestures around and their eyes follow. Sounds of the water trough and the sandpit and so forth are heard.*]

Some of the children are looking after Tommy the Tortoise and Charleene the Skink. Some of the ... Shane! Give Charleene back to Tracy, please.

[*Pause.*]

Some of the children play in the sandpit. Stavros, don't eat the sand, darling. Some cut out cardboard faces or birthday cards. There's lots of things to do. Now ...

[*They move a pace back.* CLINT *needs to go to the toilet and holds his pants with one hand.*]

This is the boys' toilet.

[*Very, very tentatively* CLINT *puts his hand up to his shoulder. So tentative is he that no one notices.* THEO *shoots his hand up.*]

THEO: And I'm getting a kangaroo called 'Rocky'.

MRS WALSH: Very good, Theo, but try not to interrupt me when I'm talking, darling. This is the boys' toilet and - [*To* LEP] This is the girls' toilet. [*To the two boys*] Now, Lep doesn't understand English yet, so until Mr San gets here on Thursday - Mr San speaks Lep's language - I'll take Lep in and show her the toilet. Come on, darling.

[*Confused,* LEP *is taken off to the girls' toilet.* THEO *and* CLINT *remain.* CLINT *clutches his pants, in pain.* THEO *belches professionally and bounces. A shutter opens in the tree and* SHANE *looks out.*]

SHANE: You!

[CLINT *whips round.*]

Recess.

[*He clenches a fist threateningly.*]
ADULT VOICE: [*off*] Shane Miller!

[SHANE *disappears fast.* CLINT *is in both physical and mental pain now. There is a scream from the direction of the girls' toilets.* LEP *runs in, upset, to the surprise of the boys.* MRS WALSH *follows quickly and catches up with her.*]

MRS WALSH: It's alright, darling. It's alright.

[LEP *hugs* MRS WALSH.]

I only turned on the water tap, darling. [*To the others*] I don't think Lep has seen running water before.

LEP: *Noi. Noi, khom mmin jong now de noo day.* [*'Noi. Noi, I don't like it in there.'*]

MRS WALSH: I wish I knew what you were saying, darling. It's alright, though; you stay here with me.

[MRS WALSH *calms* LEP *down.* THEO *is unsympathetic.*]

THEO: [*pointing off*] Mrs Walsh, what does that painting say?

[CLINT *tries to get his hand up to go to the toilet.* MRS WALSH *holds* LEP.]

MRS WALSH: You don't have to worry about that yet, Theo. That's just some school rules to help you stay safe.

THEO: [*still looking at the painting*] Who's he?

MRS WALSH: That's Willy Wombat. 'I am Willy Wombat. I don't fight in school. I don't ride my bicycle in the playground. I don't play in the toilets.' We can think about that later.

[CLINT *makes an unnoticed noise of pain and clutches his pants.*]

Now I'm going to show you Mrs O'Hara's class. Lep will be going there for her special English lessons. She won't be with you Wombats all the time. But pretty soon she'll be speaking English as well as us, won't you darling?

[*She hugs* LEP. LEP *smiles.* CLINT *makes a low howl. Piss runs down his leg.*]

Oh, Clint. What's the matter, darling? Have you had an accident? Why didn't you tell me?

THEO: Mrs Walsh, you said 'Don't interrupt'.

MRS WALSH: Oh, gee! Yes, and I've been a bit of a chatterbox, haven't I? No worries, Clint. Come on, darling. We'll get you some other shorts.

CLINT: I want my mummy.

MRS WALSH: Of course you do, darling. Come on.
> [*And she leads* CLINT *off.* CLINT *walks splay-footed, and continues to leak.* LEP *and* THEO *remain.* THEO *suddenly takes a high mark.* LEP *takes a step back.*]

THEO: [*by way of explanation*] Schimmelbusch.
> [LEP *looks blank.* THEO *turns away. Blackout.*]

SECOND JOKER: [*off*] You can pick your friend. You can pick your nose. But you can't pick your friend's nose.

FIRST JOKER: [*off*] Say 'Pink'.

SECOND JOKER: [*off*] 'Pink'.

FIRST JOKER: [*off*] You stink.

SECOND JOKER: [*off*] Say 'Blue'.

FIRST JOKER: [*off*] 'Blue'.

SECOND JOKER: [*off*] You done a poo.
> [*The lights fade up on* MRS WALSH *and the kids, including* SHANE, *sitting in a circle.* THUAN *crouches in the middle with her eyes closed, her hands over her face and her head on the floor. There is a blackboard duster at her head.* MRS WALSH *stands and points to* THEO. *He rises and goes on tip toe to take the duster and resume his place. The other kids watch intently, except* CLINT, *who has only one eye on it.*]

CHILDREN:
> Doggy, doggy, who's got your bone?
> Someone stole it from your home.

> [THUAN *opens her eyes, gets up and looks slowly into everyone's face. She looks at* LEP. LEP *shakes her head.* THEO *bounces with excitement. He is a dead giveaway.*]

THUAN: [*to* SHANE] Have you got my bone?
> [SHANE *remains pokerfaced.*]
> [*Pointing at* THEO] Him!

MRS WALSH: Theo's got a name, darling.

THUAN: Theo!

THEO: [*delighted*] Yeaaah.
> [THEO *gets in the middle and puts his hands over his head.* MRS WALSH *points at* CLINT. CLINT *shakes his head, 'No'.* MRS WALSH *nods 'Yes' to him.* CLINT *stands, looks at* SHANE MILLER *and runs away.*]

MRS WALSH: Clint! Come back, darling. It's alright.
> [*Blackout. A bell rings over the following.*]

CHILDREN'S VOICES: [*singing*]
>Jingle bells,
>Batman smells,
>Robin flew away.
>Father Christmas
>Lost his knickers
>Flying TAA.

[*The lights go up on the same kids.* MRS WALSH *and* CLINT *are still absent. Only* SHANE *and* LEP *face the audience.* LEP *spoons her Cambodian lunch;* SHANE *eats his Aussie pie.* SHANE *looks at her, grimaces and makes a small dismissive noise.* SHANE MILLER *is very menacing.* LEP *stops eating and looks at her food, then at* SHANE'*s pie, then back at her own food. Blackout.*]

CHILDREN'S VOICES: [*singing*]
>Em co doi ban tay be ty xiu,
>Nhung ngon tay cua em xinh ghe.
>Day tay phai,
>Day tay trai,
>Muoi ngon tay cua em sach deu.

[*'I have two little hands,*
>Our finger are so beautiful.
>There is a right hand,
>There is a left hand,
>My ten fingers are so clean.']

[*The lights fade up.* MRS WALSH *stands in front of the class at the blackboard. On it is written 'Sport Billy and Sport Lilly went up in a balloon.' There is a drawing of a balloon and two children.*]

MRS WALSH: Yes, Shane, Clint will be coming back this afternoon. Mr Brennan's gone to fetch him. [*Looking at her writing*] 'Sport Billy and Sport Lilly went up in a balloon.' Then where did they go for an adventure?

SHANE: To the park.

THUAN: Over the sea.

THEO: We're getting a slate floor!

SHANE: To the city.

MRS WALSH: Did you say 'Over the sea', Thuan? I think they did. [*Writing on the blackboard*] 'Sport Billy and Lilly went over the sea and they saw ...' [*Chalking in some sea beneath the drawing*] What did they see? Something beginning with 'buh'.

[*She draws a 'b'.*]

That's the stalk with the ball ... ?

THUAN: At the *bottom*!

SHANE: Boat.

THUAN: Bird. Bridge.

SHANE: Brontosaurus.

MRS WALSH: Excellent.

THEO: Kangaroo.

MRS WALSH: Excellent! Lep. [*Bringing her over to the blackboard*] Bird?

[MRS WALSH *points to the air in the picture and mimes a bird flapping.*]

Bird.

[*She points to the sea, then puts out her arms to indicate a question.* LEP *takes a second, then does a waving motion with her hand.*]

[*Repeating the waving motion*] Fish! Fish! Fish!

LEP: 'Fish'.

MRS WALSH: Yes, 'Fish'. So. Excellent, Lep. Excellent, darling.

[*She returns to the board and writes.*]

Sport Billy and Sport Lilly went over the sea and they saw a brontosaurus, a bird, a bridge, a fish ...

[*A smiles spreads over* LEP'*s face.*]

A kangaroo - though what that's doing in the sea I don't know, Theo - and a boat.

[*She turns around.*]

And then what happened?

[*The lights snap off.*]

CHILDREN'S VOICES:

> Humpty Dumpty sat on a wall.
> Humpty Dumpty had a great fall.
> All the King's horses and all the King's men
> All had omelette for breakfast again.

[*The lights fade up on* MRS WALSH *as Mr Wolf. She faces the audience with the little kids poised behind her.*]

CHILDREN: What's the time, Mr Wolf?

[*She turns as the kids freeze.* CLINT *returns to school.* THEO *bounces slightly.*]

MRS WALSH: Come on, Clint, darling! Come and play with us.

[*She turns and* CLINT *joins in at the back.* MRS WALSH *faces away from the kids.*]

CHILDREN: What's the time, Mr Wolf?

[*She turns and they freeze.*]

MRS WALSH: Two o'clock. Theo, I saw you.

[THEO *is sent back.* MRS WALSH *faces the front again.*]

CHILDREN: What's the time, Mr Wolf?

MRS WALSH: Eight o'clock.

[*She turns. They freeze. She turns back.*]

CHILDREN: What's the time Mr Wolf?

MRS WALSH: *It's going home time!*

[*They all shriek with delight as she grabs for* THEO. THEO *squeals happily.* SHANE MILLER *deliberately runs into* CLINT *and he falls.* CLINT *howls.*]

Oh, Clint has had a crash. Come here, darling. [*To all*] Now you see what happens when you run in different ways? We have crashes. And Clint's not very happy about that.

CLINT: I want my mummy.

MRS WALSH: Darling, your mummy will be here to fetch you in a minute. Alright. One more go and no more crashes, please.

[*She turns to the front again and takes one step forward.*]

CHILDREN: What's the time, Mr Wolf?

[*Blackout. The end-of-day bell rings, followed by the sounds of kids. Music. The lights go up on* THEO'S DAD *at the gate with his overalls on, reading an evening newspaper.* CLINT *runs across the stage with his school bag on. He can't wait to get away from school.*]

CLINT: *Mummy!*

[THEO'S DAD *watches him go. It's a pity* CLINT *is not made of the stuff of his own offspring. He goes back to the newspaper.* LEP *enters with her plastic bag. She looks around. No one is there to meet her.* THEO'S DAD *look up, then back to his newspaper.* LEP *is confused, but waits quietly.* THEO'S DAD *looks off behind him, looks back at* LEP *and tries to point her off. This confuses her even more.* THEO'S DAD *folds and pockets his newspaper as he looks*] *around for* THEO. *He offers his hand to* LEP *and points to where she should be going. He leads her gently off.* THEO'S DAD *comes back, checks his watch and takes his newspaper out again.*]

THEO: [*off*] Sturt!

[THEO *bounces on with his school bag on his shoulders.*]

THEO'S DAD: Hey, Theo! Good?

THEO: 'S'lright.

THEO'S DAD: What you do today, Theo?

THEO: Mucked about.

THEO'S DAD: [*going to embrace him*] Hey.

[THEO *puts his arms up to fend him off.*]

THEO: Dad! I'm at big school now.

[*He bounces off.* THEO'S DAD *is hurt, then philosophical and then pleased.*]

THEO'S DAD: Son of his father. [*Raising an arm, moving off*] Theo! Theo!

[*As he exits the shutters fly open to reveal two jokers in the same house.*]

SECOND JOKER: I'm from Mars. Give me your right hand.

[*The* THIRD JOKER *takes his hand. They shake hands continuously over the following.*]

Where are you from?

THIRD JOKER: Earth.

SECOND JOKER: On Mars we live underground. Where do you live?

THIRD JOKER: In a house.

SECOND JOKER: Where do you go to the toilet?

THIRD JOKER: On a toilet.

SECOND JOKER: What do you wipe your bum with?

THIRD JOKER: With paper.

SECOND JOKER: We wipe ours with our right hand.

THIRD JOKER: [*withdrawing his hand*] Uuurgh.

[*The shutters slam. A spot reveals* LEP *and* NOI *at a migrant hostel.*]

LEP: *Khom jee wombat.* [*'I'm a wombat.'*]

NOI: Wombat?

LEP: Wombat.

NOI: *Si I noon wombat?* [*'What's a wombat?'*]

[LEP *shrugs. Not a clue. She waves her hand as she has done in class.*]

LEP: Fish.

NOI: Ah, fish.

LEP: [*pointing to herself*] Darling. Excellent.

NOI: [*Pointing to* LEP, *puzzled*] 'Darling'. 'Excellent'. *Lo Rafferty, g a net to teene,* 'mate'. *Quat teem te ne yea:* 'mate'. [*'Mr Rafferty, the man here, "mate". Always like that: "mate".'*] 'Mate', 'mate', 'mate'.

LEP: 'Mate'. 'Mate'.

NOI: [*counting slowly on her fingers*] 'Fish'. 'Mad Max'. 'Wombat'. 'Darling'. 'Excellent'. 'Australia'. 'Adelaide'. 'Migrant Hostel'.

LEP: ⎫
NOI: ⎭ [*together*] 'Mate'.

[NOI *holds up all ten fingers.*]

LEP: ⎫
NOI: ⎭ [*together*] Dow! [*'Ten!'*]

[*A new spot reveals* CLINT'S MUM *on the phone.*]

CLINT'S MUM: [*spiritedly*] Oh, Eddie, I did two weeks' washing, I've Hoovered every inch of this place, watched *The Young Doctors*, Ray Martin, I read a book ... You could see your face in this floor now, Eddie. Well, maybe you will Saturday?

[*A new spot reveals* THEO'S DAD *also on the phone.*]

THEO'S DAD: *Christos. Abo tin Afstralia. O Theos ine sto skolio.* [*'Christos. From Australia. Theo's at school.'*]

[*Pause.*]

Bravo. Xeris ti moo ibe otan irrthen exo ke biga na ton fillisso? [*'Great. You know what he said when he came out and I try to kiss him?'*] 'Dad, I'm at big school now.' *Nomizzi ine o Silvester Stallone. Berthia.* [*'He thinks he's Sylvester Stallone. Kids.'*]

[*A brief blackout. The lights fade up as* CLINT *enters without his bag. He goes to the house painted on the diorama.*]

CLINT: Maria. Maria! Are you home? Sit, Digger.

[*A shutter opens and* MARIA *appears.*]

When ya moving house?

MARIA: Saturday.

CLINT: Ya coming out?

MARIA: I've got homework from my new school.

CLINT: I want to come to that school with you.

MARIA: I've got to finish this. [*Showing a big painting*] Look.

CLINT: Aw, come on! Who did that?

MARIA: Rod.

CLINT: Rod?

MARIA: Yeah. Rod.

CLINT: Who's Rod?

MARIA: He's come and sit next to me at my table. He's in Grade *Two*. See ya.

> [*And she closes the shutters.*]

CLINT: Mum! Mum!

> [*He runs off. Blackout. Children's voices recite a Khmer rhyme. The lights fade up on* MRS WALSH's *class. She sits holding* LEP. THEO, CLINT, SHANE *and* THUAN *sit on the floor.*]

MRS WALSH: Shane, Theo listened to your show and tell.

SHANE: He didn't. He was bouncing.

MRS WALSH: [*to* THEO] Go on, darling.

> [THEO *opens his school bag and rapidly takes out a series of items.*]

THEO: This, um ... [*Taking out a book*] I got for Christmas ... I think it was from my Dad. [*Taking out a toy car*] This is Ayrton Senna's car that he won the Grand Prix. That says 'McLaren'. [*Taking out a scarf*] This says 'Sturt'. [*Taking out a toy kangaroo*] This is Rocky.

MRS WALSH: That's lovely, Theo. Does Rocky look after you in the night time?

THEO: Yeah. He does.

MRS WALSH: Good. Clint, have you got anything to show us?

> [CLINT *shakes his head.*]

Well, do bring something in tomorrow if you want to, darling. [*Indicating* LEP's *plastic bag*] Lep, have you got anything to show us, darling?

> [LEP *hangs onto her bag.*]

I don't want to take it, darling. [*Pointing at* THEO's *things*] Show? Like Theo.

> [*Pause. They watch. No response.* MRS WALSH *turns to* THUAN. *As she speaks,* LEP *opens her bag.*]

Thuan, do you -

THUAN: [*interrupting*] Lep wants to.

MRS WALSH: Well, I wonder what LEP *has to show us.*

> [LEP *rummages in the bag to get things in the right order. She brings out a pair of adult-sized home-made Cambodian sandals. The soles are made from car tyres, with string laces.* LEP *lays them on the floor some distance from where she was sitting.*]

That's very clever, whoever made them. But they're much too big for you, darling.

> [LEP *takes out a very ragged Cambodian straw hat. She lays it on the ground some five feet in front of the sandals.*]

That's a very interesting hat. [*To the class*] Who's do you think it is? It's much too big for Lep, isn't it?

> [*The class doesn't know.* LEP *gets out a ragged Asian dress. She lays it lengthwise between the shoes and the hat to create a human shape.*]

LEP: *Makyom.* ['*Mother.*']

> [LEP *points to the human shape she has made, then to* MRS WALSH.]

MRS WALSH: What, darling?

THUAN: She says that's her mother and you're her mother.

MRS WALSH: What?

THEO: No. *Like* her mother.

SHANE: She hasn't got a mother.

LEP: 'Mother'.

SHANE: She hasn't got a mother.

MRS WALSH: Shane! Lep had a mother, didn't you darling? And thank you very much for showing us her things. I think we ought to give Lep a big clap.

> [*The kids start to clap.* SHANE *doesn't know why.* MRS WALSH *claps, then* LEP *also.*]

Thank you, darling.

> [MRS WALSH *turns away to wipe her eyes.* SHANE *gives* LEP *a vicious dig.* LEP *tries to stop herself crying. Blackout.*]

Mr Brennan! Mr Brennan!

> [*The lights fade up to reveal* MRS WALSH *at the window. She calls off to* MR BRENNAN *in the yard.*]

Oh, Mr Brennan, Clint's run away again. I'm teaching ... I know it's the Cup; I'll let you know if your horse wins. Pel Mel. The favourite. Okay ... Sorry.

[*Blackout. Music. The lights fade up. The diorama is gone and* CLINT'*s garden is revealed.*]

CLINT: [*off*] Mum! Mum! Where are you? Mum!

[*He wanders on and takes off his school bag.*]

Where is she, Digger? Mum! Come on, Digger, you sit. Now roll over. Good boy.

[*Playing with the dog he sits and opens his bag.*]

Right, you sit and you can have a Craig McDermott chip.

[*He takes the packet out of his bag and offers it to the invisible dog.*]

Good boy.

MR BRENNAN: [*off*] Clint!

[CLINT *looks around for a means of escape. He gets up to run to the wall, but realises he can't get over it. He tries another way, but winds up stranded centrestage.* MR BRENNAN *enters, jacket over one arm.*]

MR BRENNAN: There you are, Clint.

CLINT: [*very softly, determined*] I'm not coming.

MR BRENNAN: Why's that, Clint?

CLINT: I'm going to Maria's school.

MR BRENNAN: Oh. I see. Over in the port. Ah. Long way. Is your mum in?

[CLINT *shakes his head.* MR BRENNAN *bangs his own head: he has forgotten something.* CLINT *looks curiously at him.* MR BRENNAN *notices.*]

MR BRENNAN: You know what day it is Sunday?

[CLINT *shakes his head.*]

Mums' Day.

CLINT: [*very surprised*] Ya got a Mum, Mr Brennan?

MR BRENNAN: Yes.

CLINT: Oh.

MR BRENNAN: She lives in Victoria, actually. Last mail five-thirty. Thanks for reminding me, Clint. Is your dad in?

CLINT: Haven't got a dad. Not here. We've just got Eddie.

MR BRENNAN: Ah.

[*He sits.*]

Nice garden, Clint.

CLINT: You're sitting on Digger!

[MR BRENNAN *looks under himself.*]

MR BRENNAN: Who?

CLINT: My dog.

MR BRENNAN: [*moving*] Sorry, Digger. Lovely coat. What sort?

CLINT: 'S like a lamb colour.

MR BRENNAN: Ah. [*Stroking Digger*] 'Little lamb, who made thee? Dost thou know who made thee?'

CLINT: Uh?

MR BRENNAN: [*taking out a cigarette packet*] Clint ... ?

CLINT: You shouldn't do that.

MR BRENNAN: This? Oh. No. [*Putting the packet away*] Clint, do you want to walk to school with me?

[CLINT *shakes his head.*]

Come on, Clint. We can find out who won the Cup.

CLINT: Uh? I know.

MR BRENNAN: You what?

CLINT: They were shouting it. [*Pointing*] At the pub.

MR BRENNAN: Well, who won? Clint?

CLINT: Em. Forget. Pe ... Pal, er ...

MR BRENNAN: Pel Mel?

CLINT: Yeah. Pel Mel.

MR BRENNAN: *Clint!* [*Taking out money*] Clint, that deli on the corner: they sell really good icy poles?

CLINT: Yeah. Munchies. Seventy-five cents.

MR BRENNAN: Get two. Get three. One for Digger. And a Mothers' Day card. A nice one. And a stamp.

[*He gives* CLINT *five dollars.* CLINT *takes it, unsure whether* MR BRENNAN *is serious.*]

Now. I'm having a party.

[CLINT *goes.* MR BRENNAN *sits.*]

Sorry, Digger.

[*He moves. Pause. He becomes more serious.*]

What are we going to do about Clint, Digger? This can't go on. Three times. There's a main road there. Hmmm.

[CLINT *makes an aeroplane noise off, then enters with three iceblocks, a card and a stamp.*]

Thanks, Clint. That was fast.

[CLINT *holds out all three, plus the card, and gives change.*]

[*Taking one*] You help Digger out if he can't manage his.

[*Pause. They unwrap their iceblocks.* CLINT *nods.*]

CLINT: I'm not going to school.

MR BRENNAN: Clint, you're a big bloke. You've been at school a week, right? What can I do about this?

> [*As he eats his iceblock,* MR BRENNAN *takes* LEP'*s margarine-container lunch box from his jacket pocket.* CLINT *takes it.*]

CLINT: It's Lep's.

> [CLINT *opens it.*]

MR BRENNAN: Yeah.

> [*He starts to write on his card.* CLINT *opens the box: it's full. He smells the contents.*]

CLINT: Ughhh. D'ya find it?

MR BRENNAN: Yeah. [*Writing*] 'To the best mum ...'

CLINT: Where?

MR BRENNAN: On the oval. Did you see what Lep had for lunch today, Clint?

CLINT: No.

MR BRENNAN: [*writing*] 'In the world.' Looks like she didn't eat anything, doesn't it?

> [CLINT *nods.*]

> Poor little kid's in Australia, she can speak about three of our words, she sees we eat different food, she sees we don't like *her* food ... she wants to fit in. So ...

> [*He mimes throwing the food over a fence.*]

CLINT: Will she die?

MR BRENNAN: No, no, no, no. But how am I going to help her, Clint? [*Deeply puzzled*] What would help her, do you think, Clint?

> [CLINT *considers this as he sucks on his iceblock.* MR BRENNAN *seals his card.*]

CLINT: A mate.

MR BRENNAN: You reckon? I don't know. You reckon?

> [CLINT *nods.*]

> Hmmm. You know, Clint, you might be right. [*Looking at his iceblock*] Good these. [*Back with the subject at hand*] I'm too old. Maybe someone the same age. Hmmm. I wonder. [*Looking up*] There's your mum back. Look, Clint, I'll go and have a little talk with your mum. Don't worry about anything. I'm going to give your advice a little think,

Clint. Hope I see you tomorrow. A mate, you reckon? Hmmm. But who?

[MR BRENNAN *goes, still sucking on his iceblock.* CLINT *looks after him, then has a little think as the lights fade to blackout. Music. The school bell rings as the lights go up on a diorama of the school footy oval. The word 'Footy' is stuck to the backdrop. There is a kangaroo on the oval in Sturt colours, with the word 'Sturt' on his guernsey.* LEP *enters with* NOI, *who hands her the plastic airport bag, kisses her and goes.* LEP *looks in the bag, takes out her margarine container and throws it over the wall. The bell continues to ring. She goes into school.*]

CLINT'S MUM: [*off*] Clint, stop pulling!

CLINT: [*off*] Come on, Mum.

[*Enter* CLINT *with school bag, pulling his* MUM.]

CLINT'S MUM: Now are you sure you want to go to school today, Clint?

CLINT: [*looking around the oval*] Yep.

CLINT'S MUM: If you're feeling crook we could go -

CLINT: [*interrupting*] Bye, Mum.

[CLINT *rushes into school, still scanning the oval.*]

CLINT'S MUM: Oh. Okay. See ya tonight!

[CLINT'S MUM *gives a wave. Pause. She turns for home without enthusiasm. The bell keeps ringing.*]

MRS WALSH: [*off*] Clint, aren't you making a card for your mum, darling?

[CLINT *enters.*]

CLINT: Minute. I'm taking Charleene for a walk.

[*He pretends Charleene the skink is under his shirt and starts to look around.*]

MRS WALSH: [*off*] Theo, where are you going, darling?

THEO: [*off*] Brmmm-mmm.

[CLINT *continues his search.* THEO *enters, curious.* CLINT *finds the container and opens it.* THEO *approaches with his fingers to his nose.*]

Uuurgh.

[CLINT *turns and stands strong.* THEO *stops, then belches: a challenge.* CLINT *belches back: he won't be intimidated. They repeat the exchange.*]

MRS WALSH: [*off*] Clint! Theo! Where are you?

[*Pause, then* CLINT *moves off with a final burp that says 'Don't interfere'.* THEO *doesn't.* CLINT *goes.* THEO *follows.*]

THEO: Brmmm-mmm!

[*It is unclear whether any connection between them has been made. They themselves don't know.*]

CHILDREN: [*singing*]

    Cai nha la nha cua ta,
    Ong co ong cha lap ra.
    Chau con ta gin giu lay
    Muon nam voi nuoe non nha.

    [*'The house is mine,*
    The ancestors built it up.
    We have to keep it
    Forever and ever with our country.'*]

[*The lights fade up to reveal a new diorama with the words 'Mrs Walsh's class' stuck to it. The kids in the picture have Mothers' Day cards.* MRS WALSH, LEP, THUAN *and* SHANE *set up the classroom. Two small tables pop up from the floor. A small pile of coloured card is put on the floor.* LEP *sits at one table looking at a book about Old King Cole.* THUAN *sits at the other cutting a shape into a pink Mothers' Day card. Near the pile of cards,* SHANE MILLER *also cuts.* MRS WALSH *faces away from them.* LEP *looks at what* THUAN *is doing.*]

THUAN: Mothers' Day. Sunday.

    [LEP *nods.*]

LEP: Mother?

MRS WALSH: [*calling off*] Clint! Theo!

    [*Unseen by* MRS WALSH, LEP *gets up and goes to get a piece of card. As she reaches for it,* SHANE *puts his foot on the pile.* LEP *returns to her table.* MRS WALSH *looks around, but there is no indication that anything is wrong.*]

That's going to be beautiful, Thuan. Alright, Lep? Like your new book?

    [LEP *nods.* MRS WALSH *turns away again.*]

Clint! Theo! Come on, darlings. Put Charleene back in the tank and come and make your cards.

[THEO *enters looking over his shoulder.* LEP *is close to tears and looks at* THUAN. THEO *picks up a piece of card and heads for* THUAN'*s table.* SHANE MILLER *stops him.*]

THEO: Mrs Walsh!

SHANE: [*to* MRS WALSH] I've finished.

[CLINT *enters. There's no sign of the lunch box.* THEO *watches* CLINT. MRS WALSH *goes to* SHANE.]

MRS WALSH: Well done, Shane!

[CLINT *sits opposite* LEP. MRS WALSH *moves to* THUAN *and* THEO, *who continues to watch* CLINT.]

[*Appreciatively, looking at* THUAN'*s card*] Hmmm.

[CLINT *puts the margarine-container lunch box on the table.* LEP *looks at it.*]

[*To* THUAN] Who's that sitting beside you, Thuan?

THUAN: Buddha.

THEO: Who's Buddha?

MRS WALSH: Another person like Jesus.

[MRS WALSH *turns to* THEO'*s card.* LEP *pushes the lunch box away.*]

CLINT: [*grabbing the box*] No! Tucker. Good. No die.

MRS WALSH: [*to* THEO] That's the way. Very good, Theo.

CLINT: [*to* LEP] Tucker. Good.

MRS WALSH: Everything alright?

[CLINT *nods and starts to get up.* LEP *wipes her eyes.*]

THUAN: Mrs Walsh, can you write 'Mother'?

MRS WALSH: You try, darling. I'll watch.

CLINT: [*to* LEP, *annoyed*] Always crying! Struth.

[MRS WALSH *takes the pen from* THUAN *and writes for her.*]

THUAN: [*watching*] 'Mother'.

LEP: [*pointing to the card*] Mother.

[CLINT *looks around and sees* LEP'*s problem.*]

CLINT: No.

THUAN: Mrs Walsh, are you Buddha?

MRS WALSH: No, darling, I'm Jesus Christ.

CLINT: [*to* LEP] No. No good. You no mother, see?

THUAN: [*to* MRS WALSH] You don't come back here when you die?

MRS WALSH: No, darling.

THUAN: [*sadly*] Ahhh.

MRS WALSH: [*to* LEP] What's the matter, darling?

CLINT: She wants to make a Mothers' Day card, but she can't, can she?

[LEP *is upset.*]

SHANE: She hasn't got a mother!

MRS WALSH: Alright, Shane!

CLINT: [*to* LEP] Can't make one, can you?

[LEP *is upset and confused.* MRS WALSH *moves to her.*]

MRS WALSH: Darling, don't cry. It's alright. Oh, golly. We'll finish these.

[THUAN *looks at* LEP *and gets up to go to the pile of cards.* MRS WALSH *comforts* LEP. *Out of* MRS WALSH'*s view,* SHANE *puts his foot on the cards.* THEO *moves from his table and approaches the cards with determination.* SHANE *digs him. As* MRS WALSH *turns around,* THEO *throws a punch at* SHANE *which connects.*]

Theo!

[THUAN *picks up a card.*]

THEO: [*very quickly*] She was getting a card for Lep and he put his foot on it and I tried to get it and he digged me!

SHANE: [*with equal passion and conviction*] I didn't! He put his hand out for it and I was going to help and I accidentally touched his arm accidentally.

THEO: Awww!

MRS WALSH: Theo!

[THUAN *gives the card to* LEP.]

No, we'll stop there. We'll not have fights over these cards. And Lep can't make one, so she's upset, which I should have thought of. It's not very fair at all.

SHANE:⎫
CLINT: ⎬ [*together*] Awww.
THUAN:⎭

MRS WALSH: No!

[*She returns to her desk and gestures that they finish.* CLINT *sees* LEP *with the blank card.*]

CLINT: No, Thuan. Her mum's dead. She can't give it to her.

THUAN: She can! Mrs Walsh! Mrs Walsh!

MRS WALSH: Yes, darling? [*To the others*] Please finish.

[THUAN *goes to* MRS WALSH *and whispers in her ear as* LEP *looks helplessly at her card.*]

SHANE: [*to* THEO, *under his breath*] Pervert!

THEO: [*to* SHANE, *under his breath*] Dickhead!

MRS WALSH: [*to* THUAN] Really? [*Calling*] Shane! Theo! [*To* THUAN] I didn't know that. Yes. We'll need matches. Go and ask Mr Brennan: he smokes.

[THUAN *nods and exits.*]

Clint, would you find some pencils for Lep, please?

CLINT: [*standing*] Why?

SHANE: Eh?

MRS WALSH: Thank you.

[MRS WALSH *turns and behind her back* THEO *points at* SHANE. *They are on a collision course.* CLINT *makes a fold in* LEP'*s card.*]

CLINT: Are we making a card for Lep, Mrs Walsh?

MRS WALSH: [*coming over*] Yes.

LEP: Mother.

MRS WALSH: [*to* CLINT, *taking up a pen*] 'To my mother'?

CLINT: Yes.

SHANE: [*sotto voce*] Stupid!

[MRS WALSH *writes.* THUAN *arrives with a metal bin and a box of matches. Everyone but* LEP *and* MRS WALSH *are surprised.* THUAN *sets the bin on the table.*]

MRS WALSH: 'To my mother, from Lep.'

[MRS WALSH *gets up and gives the card to* LEP.]

Right, can everyone come round for a few minutes, please?

SHANE: Why?

MRS WALSH: Lep?

[MRS WALSH *directs* LEP *to put the card in the bin as the others gather round in a semicircle.* THUAN *hands the matches to* MRS WALSH.]

CLINT: What ya doing?

[SHANE *pushes in next to* LEP. CLINT *eases himself between them, putting* SHANE *to the side of the group. He connects with* THEO.]

SHANE: Hey!

MRS WALSH: Right, if we just have quiet for a little five seconds.

[MRS WALSH *lights a match and puts it to the card. The smoke starts to rise. Music.*]

SHANE: This is stupid, Mrs Walsh.

MRS WALSH: No, it's not stupid, Shane. You'll all be taking your cards home to your mums this afternoon and this is a way Lep can send a card to her mother.

[THEO *slips in between* CLINT *and* SHANE *so that* SHANE *is on the end of the line.*]

CLINT: How?

MRS WALSH: [*indicating the smoke*] Buddha is taking the card up to Lep's mother.

CLINT: ⎫
THEO: ⎭ [*together*] Yeh?

[*They watch.* SHANE *tries to throw a punch at* LEP. THEO *catches his arm and holds it tight.* SHANE, *caught in mid-punch, can't cry out. Silently they watch as the smoke rises. The music swells and the lights fade to blackout. There is lots of shouting and noise as children go home from school. The lights fade up on the same location.* LEP, THEO *and* CLINT *sit on the table with their school bags on.* THEO *and* CLINT *have Mothers' Day cards in their hands.*]

THEO'S DAD: [*off*] Theo. Where are you?

[*Pause.* THEO'S DAD *enters.*]

Ah. Theo.

[THEO *gets up and shows his dad his card.*]

Beautiful. Your mother will love. Okay. Let's go and show her. What else you do today?

THEO: [*bouncing out*] Mucked about.

[*They go. Pause.*]

NOI: [*off*] Lep. Lep.

[NOI *enters.*]

Lep.

[LEP *goes to* NOI, *then turns to indicate* CLINT.]

LEP: Mate. Clint. Theo.

NOI: Ah, mate! *La aw hi. Da jung tow.* [*'That's good. Let's go.'*]

[*And they go.* CLINT *sits and looks at his card. His mum appears behind him. She's had a bad day. She comes in.* CLINT *sees her. He hands her the card. She takes it and looks at it, then puts her arms around him, very moved.*]

CLINT'S MUM: It's beautiful, Clint. D'you have a good day?

[*Pause. He doesn't look at her.*]

CLINT: 'S alright.

CLINT'S MUM: I missed you, Clint.

> [CLINT *is embarrassed. She holds him as the music rises and the lights fade to black. The lights fade up on* LEP *and* THEO *as they close the doors of the diorama. Again the painting of* CLINT, LEP *and* THEO *holding hands is revealed, with a kangaroo and* MRS WALSH *in the background. Stuck to the picture are the words 'Our Story' and 'The End'. The music continues.*]

CHILDREN: [*off, singing*]

> A sailor came to I love you
> To see what he could I love you,
> But all that he could I love you
> Was the bottom of the deep blue I love you.

> [*The lights fade to black. The cast enter and sing a further verse of 'A sailor came ...' They then take their curtain call. They wave to the kids and exit.*]

THE END

BEAUTY AND THE BEAST

Beauty and the Beast was first performed by Magpie Theatre at the Odeon Theatre, Norwood, Adelaide, on 5 March, 1988 with the following cast:

RYAN	Michael Habib
PADDY	Tom Considine
BEAUTY	Claudia LaRose
BRIDIE/BALLARAT	Annabel Giles
BERNADETTE/SHEEP	Sharon LeRay
THE BEAST/BALLARAT/ FITZROY	Tim Aris

Directed by Chris Johnson
Designed by Julie Lynch
Music by Alan John
Lighting by John Comeadow
Harpist Moira Lawry

CHARACTERS
RYAN, a former gold digger turned prosperous merchant
PADDY, an old mate who lost an arm on the goldfields
BEAUTY, RYAN's second daughter
BRIDIE, his eldest daughter
BERNADETTE, his youngest daughter
THE BEAST, with the head and paws of a kangaroo
BALLARAT, a stray sheep dog rescued by BEAUTY
A SHEEP
FITZROY, Mayor of the city

SETTING
Australia in the eighteen-sixties. The action begins in an elegant room in a house in a city port, then moves to a sheep station and the house of The Beast amid wild and unexplored bush country.

NOTE:
Songs used throughout the play are traditional, with music by Alan John available on application. The publishers believe that no copyright infringement has occured in reproducing the songs here, but if an infringement has inadvertently been committed the owner is invited to contact the publisher for prompt acknowledgement.

Above: Michael Habib as Ryan. Below: Claudia La Rose (centre) as Beauty, Sharon Le Ray and Annabel Giles as her sisters. Magpie Theatre Production. Photo: Eric Algra.

ACT ONE

SCENE ONE

An elegant, gas-lit room in a large house overlooking the harbour, night. Music echoes the sound of the storm at sea outside. The room contains a globe, a chair, a chandelier a vase and a pedestal. The merchant, RYAN, *watches the sea through a large seaman's telescope mounted on a tripod. Into this comes the first distorted verse of the song.*

SOUTH AUSTRALIA IS MY NATIVE HOME

VOICES: [*singing*]
South Australia is my native home,
Heave away! Heave away!
South Australia is my native home,
I am bound for South Australia,
Heave away! Heave away!
Heave away you ruler King,
I am bound for South Australia.

[PADDY *enters.*]

PADDY: Nothin'?

RYAN: Waves as high as houses, but no sail.

PADDY: Well will you not eat somethin', mate, and rest? I'll keep nit.

RYAN: How can I rest, Paddy?

PADDY: Ryan, I'll bet Dublin to a brick The Adelaide and all her London cargo will be bobbin' there in the harbour within a week. [*Taking out money*] There, a quid.

RYAN: If me ship does a perish, mate, I'll not own a quid.

PADDY: Then eat while yer can, yer awkward man!

[BEAUTY, RYAN'*s second daughter, enters.*]

BEAUTY: Paddy, have you seen Ballarat?

[*She notices* RYAN.]

Father!

PADDY: Beauty, I -

BEAUTY: [*to* RYAN, *interrupting*] Not again watching the ocean all night?

PADDY: He has.

RYAN: Ballarat?

BEAUTY: [*calling, looking about*] Here boy! [*Shaking her head at* RYAN] Father!

PADDY: [*to* RYAN] Dog.

RYAN: Dog? We have no dog.

BEAUTY: [*calling*] Ballarat!

PADDY: Yer have since this afternoon, mate.

[RYAN *returns to his perusal of the sea.*]

BEAUTY: Father. Rest!

PADDY: Little tousel-haired bushranger of a thing. Fella throws this hemp sack into the harbour. Sack which starts to yelp ...

RYAN: Beauty.

BEAUTY: [*still looking*] Poor little drowning thing.

PADDY: In she jumps, Mademoiselle, in her Sundays and pulls out the little bludger.

BEAUTY: [*calling*] Ballarat.

[RYAN *notices something on the ocean.*]

RYAN: Shhh.

PADDY: What is it, mate?

RYAN: There on the harbour wall. The waitin' wives and mothers of our sailor boys: they saw somethin and gave a shout.

BEAUTY: The Adelaide.

[*Pause. Beauty looks at* PADDY, *then* RYAN's *eye comes away from the telescope.*]

RYAN: A fleck of dawn mist. No sail.

PADDY: Then Beauty, will yer tell your da that he can't go another night without a feed.

BEAUTY: Father.

PADDY: [*to* RYAN] We're naggin' yer, Ryan, if yer hadn't noticed.

BEAUTY: [*insistently*] I'll watch.

[*Pause.* RYAN *nods.*]

PADDY: Then why wouldn't yer do it for yer old digger mate?

BEAUTY: Paddy! [*Calling*] Ballarat!

PADDY: [*to* RYAN] There's a fine plump roast chook for yer on the kitchen table. And johnny cake too.

RYAN: [*heading off*] Shout me straight, Beauty, any sign of sail.

[RYAN *exits.*]

PADDY: I swear your da, Beauty, is the most awkwardest man in the colony.

[BEAUTY *goes to the telescope.*]

BEAUTY: Nothing. Come home, Adelaide.

PADDY: Beauty, has not your da had his ship ten days late before and come safe home?

[*He goes to the globe and points to various points.*]

Driven off course by a squall or two here. Becalmed as happens often here. Driven too far south here. No. Any day now we'll look down and see those four tall masts and a rich cargo.

[*Unseen,* BALLARAT *the dog enters with a chook clamped in his jaws. The others don't see him as he scuttles for a hiding place behind a chair at which to eat.*]

BEAUTY: [*looking through the telescope*] Paddy, you should insist Father rests.

PADDY: Insist? Where did insistin' ever get me with yer da? [*Indicating his missing arm*] When I lost this with that rock fallin' on me at Ballarat, did I not insist then? 'Mate, ya don't need a one-armed Irish nuggetter holdin' ya back. Forget about me!'

BEAUTY: [*calling*] Ballarat!

[BALLARAT *thinks about announcing himself, but having much of the chook still to eat he thinks better of it and hides again.* BEAUTY *continues to watch the ocean.*]

PADDY: That dog is a thief, Beauty. Did yer not see it in his sly eyes?

BEAUTY: Paddy, he'll make a fine dog.

PADDY: And did he listen, yer da? He digs twelve days and nights straight while I'm havin' me arm sawn off.

BEAUTY: But he struck it, didn't he Paddy? And made his fortune.

PADDY: I'm not whippin' the cat, Beauty. He did. Your man struck it.

THE INDICATING ROCK

[*Singing*]
> For at eighty feet he's struck it,
> And its nearly two feet wide.

BOTH: [*singing*]
> And the lucky Ryan lit his pipe
> And viewed the reef with pride.
>
> He could see the gold as plainly
> As the hands upon a clock
> And he blessed the day he sunk upon
> The Indicating Rock.

[*As they sing,* RYAN *enters and also fails to notice* BALLARAT.
BEAUTY *shakes her head to indicate no luck at the telescope.*]

ALL: [*singing*]
> Come all you jolly diggers
> And sons of Irish soil
> Who have come to dig on Ballarat
> And tried to make a pile.
> Your labour is as constant
> As the pendulum of a clock
> And you pay such great attention
> To the Indicating Rock.

PADDY: Did I not tell ya yer da was starvin', Beauty? He's finished off his chook and johnny cake in two minutes.

RYAN: I've eaten nothin'.

PADDY: In the kitchen! On the table.

RYAN: There's nothin' there but an empty plate, Paddy.
> [*Pause.*]

PADDY: Bushranger! He's started his life of crime.

BEAUTY: Oh, no.

PADDY: The little thief!

BEAUTY: Paddy.

RYAN: The dog?

PADDY: It's execution dock for the mongrel.

BEAUTY: No.

RYAN: [*indicating the telescope*] Keep nit, Beauty. I'll save the dog for yer.

BEAUTY: You're all bark, Paddy. You'll come to love that dog.

PADDY: Sure I will not.
RYAN: Paddy, calm yourself!

[PADDY *and* RYAN *exit.* BEAUTY *goes to the telescope and watches through it.* BALLARAT *continues to demolish the chook.*]

BEAUTY: Come home, Adelaide. Come home.

[BALLARAT *eats noisily behind her. At last she hears the sound and turns, aghast.*]

Ballarat! You naughty ... No. No.

[BALLARAT *comes out from behind the chair with the chook still in his jaws. Thinking that* BEAUTY *has a game in mind, he rolls on the floor to be rubbed.*]

Ballarat, have you no shame? Here, make yourself scarce, mister.

[BEAUTY *shakes her head at the mutt in despair, then goes back to the telescope. She looks back at the satisfied* BALLARAT, *then looks in the lens. She draws back, rubs her eyes and looks again.*]

Sail. Sail! Is it? Shhh. Wait. There again. Masts. One, two, three, four. [*Shouting*] Father! Father!

[*She gets up and kisses* BALLARAT.]

Oh, Ballarat, we're saved!

[RYAN *rushes in, followed by* PADDY *with a meat chopper.* PADDY *sees* BALLARAT *and the half-eaten chook.*]

PADDY: You! Thief!
RYAN: Paddy! [*To* BEAUTY] What is it, Beauty? That's a fair lookin' dog.
BEAUTY: There!
PADDY: The Adelaide! The Holy Mother's heard you, mate! [*Turning to* BALLARAT] Bushranger, bark your prayers.]
BEAUTY: No! [*To* RYAN] Sou' sou' west.
RYAN: [*going to the telescope*] Oh, Beauty.
BEAUTY: Paddy! He's brought us luck.
PADDY: Beauty, he's no good to gundy. And never will be.
RYAN: [*looking through the lens*] Shhh. It's her. Paddy. Fetch me coat, mate.
PADDY: [*heading off*] Ya feed!
RYAN: Let the mongrel have the chook. I must run to the harbour and greet me captain. See the women wavin', Beauty? They've sighted their sailor boys.

[PADDY *exits.*]

Oh, Beauty. I thought we'd be on the street again, girl.

[*They embrace.*]

The crew of The Adelaide are our guests tonight and'll want a good Irish welcome to Australia! Wake yer sisters!

BEAUTY: We'll give them a welcome, Father!

[BEAUTY *exits as* PADDY *comes back with the overcoat.*]

PADDY: There. [*Helping* RYAN *into the coat*] Now run to yer sailor boys and I'll cook the tucker.

RYAN: Oh, mate. What a day! What a day!

[*And he exits.* PADDY *looks at* BALLARAT *and* BALLARAT *looks at him.*]

PADDY: 'Ballarat' is it? Me name's 'Paddy', not 'Mulga Bill'. One day when Beauty isn't about -

BALLARAT: [*interrupting*] Woof.

PADDY: [*raising his arm*] What?

[BALLARAT *scoots after* BEAUTY *and nearly cannons into* BERNADETTE, *the youngest daughter, as she enters.*]

BERNADETTE: Ughhh. Uncle Paddy, why all this noise? It's still dark!

PADDY: Me apologies for raisin' ya before noon, Bernadette, and yer having no experience of it.

BERNADETTE: Uncle Paddy!

PADDY: The Adelaide.

BERNADETTE: Ohhh. Uncle Paddy! At last, the news from London. Oh, and what will the ladies be wearing there this year, I wonder.

PADDY: Clothes, I reckon.

BERNADETTE: Oh!

[BRIDIE, *the eldest daughter enters arm in arm with* BEAUTY. *Both are beaming.*]

BRIDIE: Uncle Paddy, is it true?

PADDY: See for yerself, Miss Bridie.

BRIDIE: Oh, Beauty. The Adelaide and my handsome first officer, Johnny Galvin.

[BEAUTY *gives her a conspiratorial squeeze.*]

BERNADETTE: Oh, Uncle Paddy. Do you know what presents Father has for us on that ship? Diamonds?

PADDY: And why should yer be gettin' diamonds that didn't
sit up a single night with yer da, but was out gallivantin'
with rich young English fellas till ten thirty and later?
BERNADETTE: Oh, Uncle Paddy.
PADDY: Your da says he's bringin' all the officers and crew -
BRIDIE: [*interrupting, alarmed*] My Johnny can't see me like
this.
BEAUTY: Bridie, Mr Johnny Galvin, First Officer, has been
six months at sea. He'll want a wash himself before he
comes to pay his compliments to you.
[BRIDIE *calms and hugs* BEAUTY *again.*]
PADDY: Peace, will youse! He wants youse all to dress up in
yus finest and give Mr John Galvin and all them other sailor
boys an Irish welcome. While Mr Patrick Malone attends
to the menu.
BERNADETTE: [*to* BEAUTY] Oh, no. Uncle Paddy's cooking.
Beauty, will you accompany me on the piano?
[PADDY *takes out tin whistles.*]
PADDY: What the Divil is Irish about piannas? Won't some
of youse play these?
BERNADETTE: Beauty will! And Uncle Paddy will dance.
PADDY: We'll give the sailor boys an air as they troop through
the door. What do you say?
OTHERS: Oh, ye-es.
BEAUTY: And we'll play in honour of Bridie's young man.
[BEAUTY *takes the tin whistles and begins the introduction.*]
BRIDIE: Thank you kind Sister.
BERNADETTE: Well, I don't think Mr Galvin exceptionally
handsome.
BEAUTY: ⎫
BRIDIE: ⎭ [*together*] He is!

JOHNNY IS THE FAIREST MAN

BERNADETTE: [*singing*]
      'P' stands for 'Paddy', I suppose.
[BEAUTY *squeezes* BRIDIE *again.*]
BRIDIE: [*singing*]
      'J' for my love, 'John'.
BEAUTY: [*singing*]
      And the 'W' stands for false 'Willio'.
ALL: [*singing*]

But Johnny is the fairest man.

Johnny is the fairest man, my love,
Johnny is the fairest man,
And I don't care what anybody says,
For Johnny is the fairest man.

[BEAUTY *plays a chorus and* BERNADETTE *claps as* BRIDIE *takes* PADDY *for a dance. The chorus ends and* BERNADETTE *grabs* PADDY *and dances with him as* BRIDIE *sings and* BEAUTY *plays.*]

BRIDIE: [*singing*]
As I went out one May morning
To take a pleasant walk.
I sat meself down upon an old stone wall
To hear two lovers talk,

To hear what they might say, my dear,
To hear what they might say;
That I might know a little more about love
Before I go away.

[*The dancing pauses and the three sisters come together.*]

BERNADETTE: [*singing*]
'P' stands for 'Paddy', I suppose.

BRIDIE: [*singing*]
'J' is for my love, 'John'.

BEAUTY: [*singing*]
And the 'W' stands for false 'Willio'.

ALL: [*singing*]
But Johnny is the fairest man.

[BEAUTY *grabs* BERNADETTE *and dances with her.*]

PADDY: [*singing*]
'Come and sit yerself beside me, dear,
Together on the green,
For it's a long three quarters of a year
Since together we have been.'

[BRIDIE *grabs* PADDY *and they all sing while the two pairs dance.*]

ALL: [*singing*]
       'No, I'll not sit by you', she says,
       'Now nor any other time,
       For I hear you've got another little girl
       And your heart's no longer mine.

       'Your heart's no longer mine, my dear,
       Your heart's no longer mine;
       For it's just three quarters of a year, no more,
       And your heart's no longer mine.'

[*The three sisters come together again. As they sing, behind them their father enters, followed by an austere, carefully dressed man:* FITZROY, *the Mayor of the city port.* RYAN *is downcast.*]

BERNADETTE: [*singing*]
       'P' stands for 'Paddy', I suppose.

BRIDIE: [*singing*]
       'J' is for my love, 'John'.

BEAUTY: [*singing*]
       And the 'W' stands for false 'Willio'.

ALL: [*singing*]
       But Johnny is the fairest ...

[*The song dies as they see the newcomers.*]

BEAUTY: Father!

BRIDIE: Your Worship.
    [*The girls curtsy.*]
Father, where are the officers?

PADDY: Mate?

BEAUTY: Father?

RYAN: I cannot speak, Beauty.

BEAUTY: The Adelaide? [*To the Mayor*] Sir?

FITZROY: Ladies, you will know that the cargo sent from London on The Adelaide was all of your father's fortune. More than his fortune, since he borrowed heavily from the city to finance it.

BRIDIE: But the city will be repaid. When the cargo is sold -

FITZROY: [*interrupting*] Ladies, The Adelaide brings no cargo.

OTHERS: What?

BEAUTY: Empty?
    [RYAN *shakes his head, unable to speak.*]

FITZROY: Your father's ship, some days off course near Java, was attacked by pirates. The Captain, knowing that he could not outrun the Javanese, the ship so laden, jettisoned the cargo to save the lives of the crew.

BRIDIE: Oh, no! My Johnny!

FITZROY: All safe.

BRIDIE: Thank God.

BERNADETTE: No cargo ...

RYAN: The Captain did his duty.

BERNADETTE: Our jewels.

BRIDIE: Bernadette!

BEAUTY: Father, what is going to happen to you?

RYAN: I've to go with the Mayor. To prison.

OTHERS: What?

FITZROY: The debt. Your father has no means.

BRIDIE: Gaol?

PADDY: Gaol? For debt? Would the city be gaolin' him if he was English? Ya going to treat him like a blue-shirt, are youse all, that's eaten off his plate?

FITZROY: It's the law, Mr Malone.

PADDY: The law for the Irish, mate. There's another for yer English.

BEAUTY: You'll not put my father in prison.

RYAN: Beauty!

BEAUTY: Mr Mayor, how much do we owe?

FITZROY: In round figures ... eight thousand pounds.

BEAUTY: Eight thousand pounds?

    [*Pause. She thinks.*]

How much will the City offer for The Adelaide?

FITZROY: What? The City does not buy ships. You must advertise an auction, and whatever it yields will be taken from the debt.

BEAUTY: Meanwhile our father is in prison? No. You can bargain for the City. The finest ship that ever came to an Australian port.

    [*The Mayor pauses, impressed with* BEAUTY'*s firmness.*]

FITZROY: The City Council would not argue if I valued The Adelaide at, say, five thousand pounds.

BEAUTY: Done! And for this house?

BERNADETTE: Beauty! Where will we live?

BEAUTY: The house?

FITZROY: This house the City would value at ... two thousand pounds.

BERNADETTE: Ohhh.

[BEAUTY *looks around at the furnishings.*]

BEAUTY: Then a thousand pounds are needed. Everything you see. Paddy, into the street. [*Putting an item of furniture on* PADDY *so that he can take it out of the room*] Fetch a dray. All this must be taken to the City Hall and sold. Sisters, help me.

[*She grabs another item.*]

BERNADETTE: No!

BRIDIE: Bernadette.

[BRIDIE *and* BERNADETTE *move to help.*]

BEAUTY: And all our jewels, sisters.

BRIDIE: ⎫
BERNADETTE: ⎬ [*together*] Nooo!

[BEAUTY *takes off a brooch or necklace of her own. Her sisters' hands go to their throats. Then* BRIDIE'*s hands come down.* BERNADETTE'*s do not.*]

BEAUTY: [*removing more jewellery*] Bernadette!

[*She goes to the others and takes their brooches from them.*] Mr Mayor, these jewels. There are more upstairs, say as many again. Would all this fetch to a thousand pound?

FITZROY: If it does not, the city will be content with this. Mr Ryan, I envy you. You have lost a fortune, but the treasure you have here makes you a rich man, sir. Ladies.

[*As the Mayor leaves,* PADDY *re-enters and grabs a piece of furniture.*]

PADDY: There's a dray comin'.

[*The girls shake their heads and pitch in.*]

BERNADETTE: But where will we live?

BRIDIE: Oh, Father!

[BEAUTY *comforts* BRIDIE. *They continue to carry furniture off.*]

BERNADETTE: We have lost everything.

PADDY: Almost everythin'.

BEAUTY: Paddy?

PADDY: Remember, mate?

RYAN: What?

PADDY: Five, six years ago. So small you took no notice. The little station that was deeded with this.

BRIDIE: Station? I'm sorry. I can't bear it.

[BRIDIE *exits, close to tears*.]

BEAUTY: Poor Bridie.

PADDY: Out station. In the north. What did they call it? 'Moongalba'.

BEAUTY: I'll get a map.

PADDY: It's the westest west, Beauty. The Never Never. No maps.

[BEAUTY *carries the last of the furniture off*.]

BERNADETTE: A house in the bush?

PADDY: House? Humpy. We'll be nothin' but stringy-bark settlers, but we'll live.

BERNADETTE: Oh, nooo.

[BEAUTY *returns*.]

BEAUTY: There. All done. But Paddy, how could we support ourselves there? We have nothing.

PADDY: Paddy didn't come away from the diggin's quite empty-handed. I have three blue backs sitting in the bank and - [*Turning to* RYAN] Nobody'll tell me how I'll spend them, neither! Ten pounds to buy sheep, and five to buy enough supplies to last us till we can shear 'em. That spent, we swag it, back of sunset. Don't we, mate?

[*Though confused,* RYAN *perks up slightly*.]

BEAUTY: North, Paddy?

BERNADETTE: Oh, nooo.

[BERNADETTE *goes*.]

BEAUTY: Poor Bernadette. The Never Never?

PADDY: Yer still got your old billy, Ryan?

THE OVERLANDERS

[*Singing*]
>   So pass the billy round, boys,
>   Don't let the pint pot stand there,
>   For tonight we'll drink the health
>   Of every overlander.

Come on, Ryan, crack hardy.

BEAUTY: Father, we can do it.

PADDY: Ballarat and Bendigo didn't beat us, mate.   This
    Moongalba won't.
BEAUTY: Will we give it a go, Father?
    [RYAN *looks at her.*]
PADDY: [*to* RYAN, *singing*]
                Come all you lads who long to roam
                And cannot live at ease at home
                And wish to cross the salt sea foam
                In foreign lands to wander.

BEAUTY: ⎫
PADDY: ⎭ [*together, singing*]
                I know a life will suit you well
                That from all others bears the bell.
                Pitch pen and ink and books to Hell
                And join an overlander.

    [RYAN'*s resistance is broken down.*]
ALL: [*singing*]
                So pass the billy round, boys,
                Don't let the pint pot stand there,
                For tonight we'll drink the health
                Of every overlander.

    [*The three of them embrace. Fade to blackout.*]

SCENE TWO

---

*A desert sheep station, day. Music. The sounds of flies and
heat. A sheep enters and eats.*

SHEEP: Baaa.
    [PADDY *enters, breathless, dressed in a slouch hat and old
    shirt.*]
PADDY: Yer wool-blind half breed, will ya stop bungin' on an
    act?
SHEEP: Baaa.
PADDY: Give up yer wig or I slit ya throat.
SHEEP: Baaa.

[PADDY *tries to cut him off, but the* SHEEP *moves away.*]
PADDY: Cottontop, who raised ya from a lamb? Paddy. Who's
been a da to yer nearly since yer old ma keeled over in the
dry? Paddy.
[*He makes another move towards the* SHEEP. *The* SHEEP
moves.]
Sundowning jumbuck, it was me. And Beauty too. Now
come and get yer haircut. It's yer wool or we starve.
[*He makes a move for the* SHEEP. *The* SHEEP *swerves and*
PADDY *falls.*]
Alright! Keep yer wool.
[PADDY *lies down on the ground as though he has given
up. The* SHEEP *looks at him. There is a couple of metres
between them.* PADDY *starts to sing. Over the following he
edges closer to the sheep and the sheep moves away. In
the end,* PADDY *gets nowhere.*]

> PADDY MALONE
> Och! Me name's Pat Malone, and I'm from
>   Tipperary.
> Sure, I don't know it now, I'm so bothered,
>   ohone!
> And the gals that I danced with, lighthearted
>   and airy,
> It's scarcely they'd notice poor Paddy Malone.
>
> 'Tis twelve years or more since our ship, she
>   cast anchor
> In happy Australia, the emigrant's home,
> And from that day to this there's been nothing
>   but canker
> And grate and vexation for Paddy Malone.

[PADDY *makes a big grab for the sheep. It moves aside.*]
> Oh, Paddy Malone, oh Paddy ohone,
> Bad luck to the agent who coaxed ye to roam.

Beauty! Ryan! Someone! Help. These woolies are white-
anting me and that's no lie.
[BEAUTY *enters, dressed in simple bush style.*]
BEAUTY: Paddy, what's all the shouting about?
PADDY: [*pointing at the* SHEEP] That.

BEAUTY: You want him mustered?

[*She gives a loud whistle.*]

PADDY: Save your breath, Beauty. Aren't they spread from here to Ninginbilli? We're up the wattle, girl. I haven't mustered a one.

[BALLARAT *enters.*]

BALLARAT: Woof.

PADDY: I mean, what we need is a dog. A proper, intelligent workin' bloke kind of a dog. Not a bludger that just chews your boots and thieves your tucker.

BALLARAT: [*to* PADDY] Woof.

PADDY: Yer do anythin' useful in yer life, Ballarat, and I'll be eatin' my hat.

BEAUTY: Ballarat!

[BALLARAT *stands still, alert.* PADDY *watches.*]

PADDY: What's he doin'?

[BALLARAT *takes a position behind the sheep and lays down.*]

SHEEP: Baaa.

PADDY: What?

[BEAUTY *whistles again.*]

BALLARAT: Woof.

BEAUTY: Now, Ballarat, when I tell you, take this one home to all the others.

PADDY: All what others?

[BEAUTY *whistles again.*]

BEAUTY: Ballarat, take him home.

[BALLARAT *drives the* SHEEP *in front of him. The two exit.*]

PADDY: I don't believe it.

BEAUTY: Believe it, Paddy.

PADDY: You said 'the others'?

BEAUTY: All mustered and penned and ready for shearing.

PADDY: By that three-pennorth of God-help-us?

BEAUTY: We shear tomorrow and sell the wool next week. Just in time. Next week there won't be a skerrick left in the house.

PADDY: So have we come through the first year, then, Beauty?

BEAUTY: We have, Paddy.

PADDY: I always had a feelin' about that dog, you know. I said -

BEAUTY: [*interrupting*] You said you'd eat your hat, Paddy.
[*Pause.* PADDY *takes off his hat, sweeps the sand off it,
looks at it, then bites into it.* BEAUTY *takes him round the
shoulders, they laugh and start to go. Music. Suddenly
they feel they are being watched. Frightened, they stop
laughing and retreat with caution, looking about.*]

SCENE THREE

The sheep station, day. BERNADETTE *enters. She holds a
parasol against the burning sun, but is otherwise much more
simply dressed than before.*

BERNADETTE: Who would believe there are so many flies in
the world. And snakes and sand. And sun. Endless sun.
[BRIDIE *enters from another direction. She looks into the
distance.*]
Do you see them watching us, Bridie?
BRIDIE: I see them.
BERNADETTE: Watching, always, and waiting. They say a
whole family was murdered at Sandy Creek last year. Our
lives.
[*Pause.*]
Bridie, we will die here.
BRIDIE: No. Someone will come for us.
BERNADETTE: They won't. If we survive the poisoned spear
and the boomerang, we will become old maids and we will
die here.
BRIDIE: No. Someone will come.
BERNADETTE: Who? If your Mr Johnny Galvin stumbled into
this God-forsaken wilderness, what would he see?
BRIDIE: Please, do not mention Mr Galvin, or it will break my
heart.
BERNADETTE: Then some other gentleman.
BRIDIE: He would see ladies.

BERNADETTE: Ladies? Look at us, Bridie! He would see poor country girls who once had white skin, now browned to leather. I am lined in the face at eighteen.

BRIDIE: Someone will come.

BERNADETTE: I hate this country. And had it not been for Beauty we would not be here.

BRIDIE: Beauty?

BERNADETTE: Yes. Beauty. She stole our jewels and our dresses. She had no right.

BRIDIE: Our father would have been in prison.

BERNADETTE: For how long? With our clothes and jewels we would have had rich husbands in a week and they would have bailed Father, no matter what the cost. I hate her.

BRIDIE: Bernadette, calm yourself. Someone will come. Some day. Perhaps not for all three of us at once, but they will come. If not today, tomorrow. If not tomorrow, then later. Someone will come. We must not go mad here.

[BRIDIE *exits*.]

BERNADETTE: We will go mad!

[BERNADETTE *cries*. RYAN *enters excitedly*.]

RYAN: My girls. Bridie! My girls, great, hopeful news. [*Calling loudly*] Beauty! Paddy! Come quickly.

BERNADETTE: What news, Father?

[BRIDIE *enters at a run*.]

BRIDIE: What news?

RYAN: Hopeful, hopeful news. [*Taking out a letter*] How hopeful is not yet clear, but -

BERNADETTE:
BRIDIE: } [*together, interrupting*] What news, Father?

[BEAUTY, PADDY *and* BALLARAT *enter at a run*. BALLARAT *jumps at the two sisters*.]

BERNADETTE: Down, wretched animal.

[BALLARAT *jumps at* RYAN *and licks*.]

RYAN: Brave Ballarat, will I tell you me news? Paddy, fetch the moke. Load enough food and water for a journey inside.

BERNADETTE:
BRIDIE: } [*together*] The city!

RYAN: [*to* PADDY] Why I'll tell you on the way.

PADDY: We'll be double dinkin' will we?

[PADDY *goes*.]

BRIDIE: Father!

BERNADETTE: The news!

[RYAN *refers to the letter.*]

RYAN: Ballarat, a letter from me old lawyer in the city. You remember the cargo lost off Java?

BALLARAT: Woof.

RYAN: He does. Good dog.

BERNADETTE: ⎫
BRIDIE: ⎭ [*together*] Father!

RYAN: That cargo was seized by the pirates who chased 'The Adelaide'. Now, months later, those pirates and their prize have been themselves captured by the Dutch.

BRIDIE: A change of fortune!

BERNADETTE: Oh, Father. Father.

RYAN: Young Ballarat. I must meet with the lawyer and try to prove that this lost cargo is mine in law.

BRIDIE: And you will, Father.

BERNADETTE: God bless the Dutch.

RYAN: Proving me claim will not be easy with the Dutch ...

BEAUTY: Father, what direction do you travel to the city?

RYAN: South's the shortest track, Beauty. Thirteen, fourteen days at most.

BRIDIE: Then lose no time, Father!

BEAUTY: Father, listen. This past year Paddy and me have talked with the drovers as they pass by here with their flocks-

BERNADETTE: [*interrupting, dismissively*] Drovers!

BEAUTY: They say no one ever goes through that region south. The black men believe it is evil. Men have gone into it and never returned.

BERNADETTE: Drovers! Black men!

RYAN: Beauty, will I not have Paddy and Ballarat for me protection?

BEAUTY: Father!

RYAN: Beauty, we will take care. Now, all me girls, if me mission to the city meets with success, what can I bring youse to make up for these months of poverty I have caused youse?

BRIDIE: Oh, Father. News of Mr Galvin.

BERNADETTE: And jewels and dresses.

RYAN: And Beauty, for you?
BEAUTY: Take the route east, Father. There are settlements.
    And you will add only three or four days to your journey.
RYAN: What can I bring yer?
BEAUTY: Bring yourself and Paddy home safe.
BRIDIE: Beauty, Father wants to bring you something. Let
    him.
    [*Pause.* BEAUTY *realises she is not going to persuade*
    RYAN.]
BEAUTY: A rose, then.
BERNADETTE: A rose? In this burning country?
RYAN: Beauty.
BEAUTY: If there are none, I'll be happy with yourself.
RYAN: Come, girls. See me to the track. Come, Ballarat. To
    the city and a change of fortune.
    [*They exit. The lights fade to blackout.*]

SCENE FOUR

---

*The wilderness, night. In the darkness, music indicates the
location. The sound of a dust storm rises. Lights fade up on*
PADDY *and* BALLARAT *huddled together with a lantern, very
cold.*

PADDY: Well, Ballarat, me last on Earth's a three-dog night
    and all I've got for company is yerself. Oh, if only the
    father had listened to the daughter. A fruitless journey.
    White-anted by the Dutch who want Ryan's cargo for
    themselves. Then returnin', our overloaded moke gives up
    the ghost. And to cap it this willy willy parts us from Ryan.
    A catalogue of misfortunes, Ballarat.
BALLARAT: Woof.
PADDY: Well, I don't know about you but me belly thinks me
    throat's cut. And Ryan has no more tucker than ourselves.
    Which is none. I fear by mornin' he'll be dead as a mutton
    chop and we'll have done a perish here.
    [*The sound of the storm becomes even more fierce.*]

BALLARAT: Woof.

[PADDY *jumps up and points to the sky.*]

PADDY: Ryan! How? The willy willy back fiercer than ever
and sweepin' Ryan through the sky like he was a feather.
Ryan! Mate!

BALLARAT: Woof. Woof.

PADDY: And what's this? Lights twinklin' in the trees like
they was guidin' Ryan to ... Can I believe me eyes? A
house? A fine house lit up like it was noon. Now that was
never there before.

BALLARAT: Woof. Woof.

PADDY: Ballarat, me nugget; this is magic, sure. Look, the
house and Ryan vanished now the both of them. Come on!

[PADDY *pulls at* BALLARAT, *but the dog resists.*]

Come on, Ballarat. Whatever magic power has Ryan in its
grip, there's only us two can save him. Though I fear we're
too late.

[*They start to go. Aboriginal music fades in, mixed with
the dust storm. The lights fade down to blackout.*]

SCENE FIVE

The house of THE BEAST, *day. The music weaves into
something brighter and more ornate as the lights come up to
reveal* RYAN *asleep in a bower of flowers. Beside him is a
bottle of wine, some bread and cheese and a serviette. Slowly,*
RYAN *wakes.*

RYAN: [*sleepily*] Paddy, where are yer? I can see nothin
through this willy willy. Paddy!

[*He wakes fully.*]

What? Am I awake or dreamin'? Tucker, and wine? Ah,
now I remember. [*Shouting*] Sir, whoever owns this palatial
house and this garden. These further gifts I'm findin' here,
are they for meself?

[*Pause. No answer.*]

[*Placing the food in his bag*] Then, sir, I'll thank yer for savin' me life last night. And as I am still far from me home, I will try to make me way there. I leave, thankin' yer.

[*He turns to go and at last sees the bower and array of flowers.*]

Another miracle. Here amidst a thousand flowers, the rose that Beauty asked me to find for her.

[*He picks the flower. The lighting changes and a frightening animal noise comes from offstage.* RYAN *sinks to the ground in fear.*]

What? Have I displeased the mysterious owner of this house? What have I done? Who's there? Who's there?

[*Slowly* THE BEAST *enters. He has the head and paws of a kangaroo, but his body is dressed in fine clothes of the period.* RYAN *can hardly look at him.*]

Sir!

THE BEAST: You have stolen from me.

RYAN: Stolen? Sir, I am no thief.

THE BEAST: You lie. You came here to rob me.

RYAN: No! Believe me, sir. Last night, in the middle of a willy willy I saw the Min Min and the lights beckonin' me towards a great house where, to me amazement, I saw such riches, beautiful paintings and statues. But I took nothin'. There were rooms furnished like you might see at Dublin Castle, gold and silver. And I took nothin'. Jewels such as me daughters asked me for, but I didn't finger a one. I took nothin' but some tucker that seemed to have been set out for me. But before I had a feed I called out, 'Whoever owns this magical house, will I eat this tucker?' There was no answer, so I ate it. Later I found a bed and, bein' bushed, called out, 'Will I sleep in this fine bed?' Again, no answer, so I slept. And now this mornin' ... If I have done wrong, here ...

[RYAN *offers the bag, but* THE BEAST *knocks it away.*]

THE BEAST: It was I who sent those lights into the wilderness for your safety. I who left food and a bed. And how do you thank me? You steal from me and for that you will die.

RYAN: Die? But what have I stolen? Good beast?

[*Silence. Slowly* RYAN *realises that it is the rose which he still holds in his hand.*]

This?

[THE BEAST *nods.*]

But your garden is full of flowers, Beast. Surely you would not kill a bloke for borrowin' one? Me daughter, Beauty, asked for such a rose.

THE BEAST: How many roses do you see among all these flowers?

RYAN: I see ... Oh, no!

THE BEAST: You think because I am dull and slow ... How many hours have I spent caring for it. To have one thing as beautiful as I am ugly.

RYAN: I meant no harm.

THE BEAST: But you have done harm! Unless there is a person willing to die in your place, prepare to die.

RYAN: What? Die in me place? [*Aside*] I will ask no one to die for me, but here is a chance to see me girls again before I die. [*To* THE BEAST] Beast, there may be such a person. Will I go to them?

THE BEAST: First you must give me your word someone will return here in one hour.

RYAN: A single hour? But -

THE BEAST: [*interrupting*] You will put on this ring and it will transport you in the flash of an eye to where you started your journey. In an hour, whoever puts on this ring will immediately be transported here. And here they will die.

RYAN: You have me word.

[THE BEAST *hands* RYAN *the ring.*]

THE BEAST: Then I will leave you.

[THE BEAST *exits.* RYAN *looks at the ring.*]

RYAN: Oh, Mary, Mother of God, if I had listened to what Beauty told me ... An hour to live. Oh, the saints preserve me.

[*As he exits, he puts on the ring and the music changes for the journey to the sheep station. A brief blackout.*]

SCENE SIX

The sheep station, day. PADDY *enters, followed by the three girls. All are miserable.*

BRIDIE: Oh, Father. Father.

BERNADETTE: [*to* PADDY] You left him to die!

BEAUTY: Bernadette!

BERNADETTE: Well, Paddy is safe and our father is dead!

BRIDIE: Bernadette. Bernadette!

PADDY: Fair shake of the dice! Ya think I dingoed in me oldest mate? The willy willy took him.

BERNADETTE: I'm sorry. Oh, Paddy. Oh, Father.

PADDY: And who says he's done a perish? We didn't find his bones.

BRIDIE: But Ballarat searched all night!

BERNADETTE: Oh, the gallant little dog. Almost dead of exhaustion in searching for our father.

BRIDIE: But the dust storm had covered up every trace of him.

BERNADETTE: Father!

BEAUTY: Dear sisters!

BRIDIE: Do you believe he could still be alive, Beauty?

BEAUTY: We must all believe.

BERNADETTE: But you don't! I see it in your eyes, Beauty.

PADDY: Girls! Girls! Your dad's as tough as fencin' wire. Don't give him away.

BERNADETTE: We are orphans! Oh, Beauty, if he had only listened to you.

    [BERNADETTE *bursts into tears again and clings to* BEAUTY.]

BEAUTY: Bernadette, what Paddy says is true. Our father is as tough as fencing wire. Perhaps, half starving, dying of thirst, he is out there somewhere near enough to hear us. Let him hear us!

DENNIS O'REILLY
    [*Singing*]
      My name is Dennis O'Reilly ..

PADDY:
BEAUTY: } [*together, singing*]

My name is Dennis O'Reilly;
From Dublin town I came ...

BEAUTY: Bridie!

ALL: [*singing*]
To sail this world all over;
I sailed the Australian main.

With my pack upon my shoulder
And a blackthorn in my hand,
To travel the bushes of Australia
Like a true-born Irishman.

When I arrived in Melbourne town
The girls all jumped with joy,
Saying one unto another,
'Here comes my Irish boy.'

[RYAN *appears behind them, looking haunted and sad, still holding the rose. The girls sense him and turn. The song stops.*]

BERNADETTE: Father! Father!

[*She runs to him.*]

BEAUTY: Father!

PADDY: Oh, mate. Y're safe.

BEAUTY: You're home, Father, home.

BERNADETTE: For ever and ever.

BRIDIE: Father. Oh, Father.

RYAN: Daughters. Daughters. Daughters. Please!

BEAUTY: What's the matter, Father?

RYAN: I've come home only to say goodbye.

BRIDIE: What?

RYAN: And see me family for the last time.

ALL: What?

RYAN: I have stolen from a great and evil beast who lives in that wilderness, and it'll cost me me life.

BEAUTY: No!

RYAN: I have given me word to return.

[*Pause. Silence.*]

It's only because the beast was willin' to allow someone close to me to die in me place that I have an hour's grace. I have deceived him so that I can say a last 'Goodbye' to youse all. That done, I must replace this magical ring and then in the twinkle of an eye I will be at his feet, ready to die.

BRIDIE: A promise to a beast? No! We won't let you.

BERNADETTE: What will become of us?

RYAN: I have given me word.

BERNADETTE: Stole what that you die for it? We will replace it. What?

RYAN: Somethin' he values more than anythin'.

BRIDIE: But ...

[*She looks at the rose.* RYAN *tries to hide it.*]

Ahhh. That!

BEAUTY: Nooo.

[BEAUTY *moans and covers her face.*]

RYAN: Oh, Beauty!

BERNADETTE: Oh, no. We are penniless orphans in the desert, Sister, for your silly request.

BRIDIE: Oh, Sister, Sister.

[BRIDIE *and* BERNADETTE *clasp each other and cry with anger.*]

PADDY: Girls, girls, don't let yer da's last memories of youse be of a blue. There's nothin' to be done, mate?

[RYAN *shakes his head.* PADDY *holds out his hands.*]

BEAUTY: Father, you say this evil beast is willing to see another come to die in your place?

RYAN: No, Beauty. No.

BERNADETTE: You did.

BEAUTY: Father, do you think I could live in this world knowing that my silly request has led to your death? Think, Father, what every minute for me would be like. Every second. I could not bear it, Father.

RYAN: Beauty!

BERNADETTE: Father, let her speak.

BRIDIE: Bernadette!

BEAUTY: I could not. I will not.

RYAN: Beauty.

BEAUTY: Let me be happy and take your place.

RYAN: Beauty. Beauty. No.

BEAUTY: You would insist on doing the same for me. Wouldn't you?

> [*Pause.* RYAN *knows what* BEAUTY *says is true. He cannot argue with her.*]

RYAN: Ohhh.

BEAUTY: Sisters. Paddy. Please. Leave us, please, to spend a quiet moment before I place that ring on my finger.

Now, Father, give me the ring and please go. Don't turn or say a word or my heart will break.

> [*Slowly, very slowly, without looking around,* RYAN *goes.* BEAUTY *picks up the rose. Fearfully,* BEAUTY *very slowly puts the ring on. The music and lighting changes.* BEAUTY *twirls in the air as she goes on the split-second journey.*]

SCENE SEVEN

The house of THE BEAST, *day.* BEAUTY *falls to the floor, her hands to her head. Kneeling, with her face close to the ground, she looks around.*

BEAUTY: Is this where I must die? Can this be the home of the cruel beast who will murder me? Rooms so light, so stately, so peaceful. Books in every language along the walls, bright, bright paintings and, below there in the garden, fountains and flowers, peacocks and water falls. How can evil live among so much light?

> [*A vicious roar comes from off. Footsteps approach.* BEAUTY *throws herself down in prayer.*]

Holy Mary, Mother of God ...

> [*The rest of the prayer is silent as* BEAUTY *keeps her head to the floor.* THE BEAST *enters angrily. He sees* BEAUTY *and his anger dies.*]

THE BEAST: A rose more beautiful than mine. You are Beauty.

> [*Pause.*]

You pray?

[*Pause. She doesn't look up.*]

BEAUTY: I do.

[*Pause.*]

Sir, what must I call you?

THE BEAST: Though it is hateful to me, I am a beast. I have no other name.

BEAUTY: Then, yes, I pray, Beast.

THE BEAST: Who do you pray for, Beauty?

BEAUTY: For myself.

THE BEAST: Whoever you pray to will surely listen, you being so beautiful.

BEAUTY: Our God does not look for outward beauty, Beast. He would hear a leper's prayer before mine.

THE BEAST: Then pray for me.

BEAUTY: I will.

THE BEAST: But first ... look at me.

[*Pause. She shakes her head.*]

BEAUTY: I am afraid.

THE BEAST: I understand. I am ugly. For what are you praying?

BEAUTY: I pray not to be murdered.

THE BEAST: Then your god has answered. Look at me.

[*Very slowly she raises her head and turns towards him. She sees him and silently a look of revulsion crosses her face. THE BEAST is hurt. From deep within him comes an animal cry of pain.*]

Ahhh.

[*He turns away. Pause. He calms himself, then turns slowly to look at her.*]

So beautiful. [*Looking at his paws*] So ugly.

BEAUTY: No. No.

THE BEAST: Mindless, slow, dull. Tell me the truth, Beauty. You find me ugly?

BEAUTY: The truth?

[*Pause.*]

I do.

THE BEAST: Ahhh. How could you not? Ahhh.

[*Pause.*]

Beauty, I wish to ask you something.

BEAUTY: Ask? Beast, this is your country, your land, your magical house. You have power over my life.

THE BEAST: I ask. I do not command. From this moment everything that you see in this house is yours to command.

BEAUTY: Then ask, Beast.

THE BEAST: You can answer 'Yes' or 'No' and I will obey.

[*Pause.*]

Can I look at you for a moment?

[*Pause.*]

BEAUTY: Yes.

THE BEAST: Thank you.

[*He looks at her closely, as if he has never seen a human being before. It is very, very close attention.* BEAUTY *is uneasy.* THE BEAST *notices and moves away, hurt.*]

I am sorry.

BEAUTY: No. No, Beast. Understand, I have never in my life seen such a creature as yourself. Take no notice of me. I know there is good in you. I know it in your giving back my life and that of my father. You suffer and yet you speak with kindness. Kindness is rare in my country.

[*The clock strikes six.*]

THE BEAST: Every evening, after you have eaten, I will return at this hour. In the meantime, everything you see in the house or in the garden is yours to enjoy.

BEAUTY: I must remain here, then?

THE BEAST: Before I go, I must ask you a question ...

BEAUTY: Ask, then, Beast.

THE BEAST: I promise no harm will follow your answer, whatever it is.

[*Pause.*]

Beauty, will you be my wife?

[*Long pause.*]

BEAUTY: No, Beast, I will not.

[*Pause. Then a deep howl comes from within* THE BEAST. *His body arches, racked with pain. He forces himself to stand straight, and bows.*]

THE BEAST: Good night, then, Beauty. Until tomorrow.

[*She nods and watches him go. As he leaves, another small, strangled cry escapes him.* BEAUTY *is left alone.*]

BEAUTY: Poor creature. Poor, poor creature.

[*The lights fade slowly on* BEAUTY. *Music. Fade to black.*]

END OF ACT ONE

ACT TWO

SCENE ONE

The house of THE BEAST, *day. Music begins in darkness, and the lights come up during the first verse of 'The Dying Stockman's Lament'. It is some weeks later.* THE BEAST *watches as* BEAUTY *sings. The rose which* RYAN *picked is in a vase, prominently placed.*

THE DYING STOCKMAN'S LAMENT

BEAUTY: A fine stalwart stockman lay dying,
            His saddle supporting his head.
            While his mates around him were crying
            He rose on his elbow and said:

    And now, Beast, the chorus!
      [THE BEAST *looks confused.* BEAUTY *goes on.*]
           'Wrap me up in my stockwhip and blanket
           And bury me deep down below,
           Where the dingoes and crows cannot find me
           In the shade where the coolabahs grow.'

[The song finishes and THE BEAST *claps enthusiastically.]*

THE BEAST: Excellent. Excellent. This will be my favourite, this sad one. What is it called?

BEAUTY: 'The Dying Stockman's Lament'. But Beast, in the chorus, you must sing too.

THE BEAST: I?

BEAUTY: You and I, dear Beast.

THE BEAST: Why?

BEAUTY: Because in a chorus everyone sings.

THE BEAST: I did not understand. Forgive me, Beauty. I am slow.

BEAUTY: The chorus.

THE BEAST: But my voice is poor.

BEAUTY: After three.

THE BEAST: Yours is beautiful. You sing.

BEAUTY: No. One. Two. Three.

    [*Both sing.* THE BEAST *does not remember all the words, and his voice is hoarse.*]

THE BEAST: ⎫
BEAUTY: ⎭ [*together*]

> 'Wrap me up in my stockwhip and blanket
> And bury me deep down below,
> Where the dingoes and crows cannot find me
> In the shade where the coolabahs grow.'

BEAUTY: Excellent, Beast.

THE BEAST: The Beast almost sings. The Beast almost sings.
[*He applauds himself. As he does so, the clock start to chime the hour of six. The clapping dies away.* BEAUTY *and* THE BEAST *are immediately uneasy. The chimes cease. Pause.*]

Beauty -

BEAUTY: [*interrupting*] Beast, wait. The hour has come and I know that you must ask me a question. And I must answer. I will. But please, Beast, a few more moments.
[*She takes off a small scarf and offers it to him. There is a pause, and he nods. He takes it and places it round his eyes. As he counts,* BEAUTY *goes behind the vase containing the rose.*]

THE BEAST: One, two, three, four, five, six, seven, eight, nine, ten.
[*Blindfolded, with paws in front of him, he starts to search for her. His hands touch the rose.*]
I have found you.
[*Still touching the rose, he takes off the scarf.*]

BEAUTY: Beast, no, you have found the rose which my father picked for me.

THE BEAST: And which brought you to me. It is as you are, Beauty. It is you. And look, still as fresh as the moment it was picked, so many weeks ago.

BEAUTY: It is.

THE BEAST: I have come to believe that I will not die until this rose dies.

BEAUTY: Beast, no more talk of death. My turn.
[*She takes the scarf and puts it on.*]
Are you hiding?

THE BEAST: I am.
[*He has not moved. He is only a metre from* BEAUTY, *to her side. He watches her.*]

BEAUTY: One, two, three, four, five, six, seven, eight, nine, ten. Ready or not, I'm coming.
> [*She slowly moves a pace, hands out.* THE BEAST *looks intently at her face as though smelling it.*]

I know where you'll be. Beneath the waterfall.
> [*She moves another pace, hands out.* THE BEAST *looks intently at her hands.* BEAUTY *takes another step.* THE BEAST *moves in front of her and holds up his paws so they will inevitably be touched by* BEAUTY. *She takes a pace and her hands touch. He sighs with joy and looks at her hands and his paws together.* BEAUTY *realises what he has done. She removes her hands and takes off the blindfold.* THE BEAST *hides his paws behind his back. An uneasy pause.*]

THE BEAST: Beauty, I have a gift for you.
> [*He takes out a hand mirror with a ribbon around it.*]

BEAUTY: [*taking the mirror*] Beast, you give me too much.

THE BEAST: In this magic mirror you will see, however far away it is, any scene your mind wishes to conjure up.

BEAUTY: Beast, thank you.
> [*Pause. She knows that the question is coming.* THE BEAST *knows what the answer will be.*]

THE BEAST: Beauty ... ?
> [*Pause. She turns away and shakes her head. A low, deep moan comes from* THE BEAST. *His body tightens. He tries to arrest the movement, and with great effort achieves it. He turns to face her.*]

[*Hoarsely*] Goodnight, then, Beauty. Until tomorrow.
> [*Slowly he goes. Another restrained sound escapes him as he exits.* BEAUTY *watches with great sadness, then picks up the mirror, but does not look into it.*]

How many times have I told myself, 'Beauty, look deeper than the skin. Look for the good that is inside. But can I? With him? Poor creature. Do I? Here he is, good, kind ... but ugly. And I shudder at even the touch of his hand.
> [*Pause. Disappointed with herself she lifts the mirror.*]

So what is it worth, any beauty of mine?
> [*She shakes her head and looks into the mirror.*]

My father!

[RYAN *enters at a distance, in a space that represents the sheep station. He is haggard, worn and in despair.*]

Father, with the sheep station behind. My sisters. Paddy! The sheep. Father, poor Father. So worn!

[PADDY *enters with a bowl of food and a skin bag.*]

PADDY: Come on, now, mate. Will yer have a feed?

[*Pause.* RYAN *shakes his head.*]

Then drink!

[RYAN *shakes his head again. He doesn't want to be bothered.*]

BEAUTY: [*whispering*] Make him do it, dear Paddy.

[PADDY *is at the end of his tether with* RYAN.]

PADDY: Aw, mate! Crack hardy. She may not be killed. We pray not. We who have never been exactly prayin' blokes, we pray every night. Trust in the Holy Mother, mate.

[RYAN *looks at* PADDY, *a scintilla of hope in his eyes. Then he turns away again.*]

Ya think y're the only one that misses the little girl? And what would herself say, seein' you thin as string? Whether she is in heaven or livin', I know what she'd say:

BEAUTY: Eat.

PADDY: 'Eat.'

BEAUTY: Please eat.

PADDY: 'Please eat.'

[RYAN *pauses, then shakes his head.*]

And what will your youngest do if you starve yourself to death? Her that hasn't got brains enough to give herself a headache.

[*Pause.*]

And what about old one-arm? Eat!

[RYAN *looks straight ahead.*]

Right. I'm tyin' the knot in, Ryan. I'll not witness two of God's creatures dyin' before me eyes.

[*With a flash of the head he turns to go. After several steps he is arrested by* RYAN'*s voice.*]

RYAN: Two? You say two? Who is dyin'?

PADDY: Who? Are you blind, mate? Are you deaf that you haven't heard the pitiful cries? Who?

[*And* PADDY *exits fiercely.*]

RYAN: Leave me to die, mate. With Beauty gone I cannot bear
to live.

[*He puts his head in his hands.* PADDY *returns with the
emaciated and pining* BALLARAT *on a string.*]

PADDY: There he stands. Can I call it standin'? Not a feed
in ten long weeks! So how can he stand? Half stands.
Weak as a sunburnt snowflake.

[RYAN *is silently shocked.*]

RYAN: Is this ... ?

PADDY: Who do you think it is? It's Ballarat.

RYAN: This?

PADDY: Have you been deaf, mate? Every night as you walk
the house callin' for Beauty, so is himself howlin' at the
self same spot where she vanished.

RYAN: Poor wretched creature.

PADDY: Howls growing weaker now. Very weak.

RYAN: So thin. So thin.

PADDY: He's thin as a fence rail, sure. All bone and skull and
waitin' for the crows. Is this the same dog that fossicked
all night in a willy willy to find you, Ryan?

[*Pause.*]

I'll take him away, but I'll not watch him die.

RYAN: Ballarat. No!

PADDY: He will die, mate. He won't touch his eats.

RYAN: Ballarat.

[RYAN *gets the food that* PADDY *brought for him. He takes
a little from the bowl and holds it out to* BALLARAT.
BALLARAT *turns away.*]

PADDY: Born awkward, like you, Ryan.

RYAN: Ballarat. You must not die.

PADDY: What? If Beauty lives? Come home and find her dog
dead? A fine thing.

[PADDY *picks up the bowl of food.*]

But he will not eat for me.

[PADDY *looks at* BALLARAT *and eats some of the food.*]

I think he's never forgive me over the matter of the chook.

[RYAN *grabs the bowl, takes a morsel and eats.*]

RYAN: Mmm ... Excellent. Excellent.

[BALLARAT *takes no notice.*]

PADDY: Again, mate. He didn't see you.

RYAN: Mmm ... Tucker. Mmm ...

[BALLARAT *looks the tiniest bit interested.*]

PADDY: He looks at yer, mate! He would not look at me.

[RYAN *eats some more.*]

And drink, mate. He has not drunk for weeks.

[RYAN *eats and drinks.*]

RYAN: Mmm ... Ballarat. Mmm ...

PADDY: Now try him, mate.

[RYAN *shows* BALLARAT *a small morsel.* BALLARAT *turns away.* RYAN *pushes it to him again.* BALLARAT *looks at it, then turns away.* RYAN *tries again. A long pause.* BALLARAT'*s nose gets nearer and nearer to it. Finally he sniffs it. They wait.* BALLARAT *eats.*]

Ohhh ... The little nugget. And keep eatin', mate. He must see you eat.

RYAN: Mmm ... Ballarat. Mmm ...

PADDY: Quickly, don't let him stop now. He has ten weeks of starvin' to make up and I've more tucker in the humpy.

RYAN: Good dog, plucky Ballarat. [*To* PADDY] Paddy, run, best meat for the dog.

PADDY: Come inside, mate. We'll feed the both of youse the best tucker this side of the Black Stump.

[PADDY *departs.* RYAN *gets to his feet.*]

RYAN: Come, Ballarat, eats. Good dog. Do ya think there is hope? Come, we must live in hope, must we not, plucky Ballarat?

BALLARAT: [*feebly*] Woof.

[RYAN *hugs the dog.*]

RYAN: Beauty's little nugget.

[*They exit.*]

BEAUTY: Oh, Father, will I ever see you again?

[*Sadly she turns away from the scene as the lights fade to blackout.*]

SCENE TWO

The house of THE BEAST, *day.* BEAUTY'*s song comes initially from the darkness. She sings spiritedly, with no trace of the sadness in the previous scene.*

THE DIGGINS-OH

BEAUTY:

    I've come back all skin and bone
    From the diggins, oh,
    And I wish I'd never gone
    To the diggins, oh.

    Believe me, 'tis no fun,
    I once weighed fifteen stone -

THE BEAST: [*interrupting*] What?

    [BEAUTY *laughs.*]

BEAUTY: Oh, yes. [*Singing*]

    But they brought me down to one
    At the diggins, oh.

    [*The lights fade up fully.* BEAUTY *beckons* THE BEAST *to sing his verse.*]

THE BEAST:

    I built a hut with mud
    At the diggins, oh,
    That got washed away by flood
    At the diggins, oh.

    I used ...

    [*Pause. He has forgotten the words.*]

BEAUTY: [*singing*]

    I used to dig and cry,
    It wouldn't do to die.

BOTH: [*singing*]

    Undertakers charge too high
    At the diggins, oh.

    [BEAUTY *smiles and claps* THE BEAST'*s achievement.* THE BEAST *bows, happy. Suddenly his paws go to his head, as though to a pain.* BEAUTY *starts.*]

BEAUTY: What is the matter, dear Beast?

THE BEAST: Something came into my head. The briefest picture and it was gone. In these clothes ... a man.

BEAUTY: A man?

THE BEAST: A man and not a beast. Could it be that I have lived another life? When I was not as I am now: ugly?
[Pause.]
No, my dull mind has played me a trick. I am a beast. Only a beast.
[The clock begins to chime six. BEAUTY *turns away.]*
Beauty, will you consent to be my wife?
[Pause.]

BEAUTY: Beast, please. Come and sit beside me.
[Pause. THE BEAST *moves to do so.]*
Beast, a hundred evenings, a hundred questions. Do you know how it pains me to give you the answer I do? When we first spoke you asked me to be honest with you. I will be honest and say that what you want will never come to be.
*[*THE BEAST *moans and turns away.]*
But now I know that I will always be your friend. Always. Could you, dear Beast, come to be content with that?
[Pause. THE BEAST *struggles with his feelings.]*

THE BEAST: I must. Look at yourself, Beast! Such ugliness has no business loving such beauty. But you do. From the first moment you saw this Beauty, you have loved her. You cannot help it.
[Pause.]
It should make you happy that she will always be your friend.
[He looks at BEAUTY.]*
It does.
[Pause.]
Beauty, promise me.

BEAUTY: Anything else, good, good friend.

THE BEAST: Promise that you will never leave me.
[Pause. She nods. This gives THE BEAST *some limited pleasure.]*

BEAUTY: Beast, you know that there is something else troubles me.

THE BEAST: I do. I was afraid to ask what it was in case I could not help.

BEAUTY: But you can. Beast, in this wonderful mirror I have seen my poor father sickening. Beast, he does not know if I am alive or dead. I long to see him and reassure him. I will die if I cannot.

> [THE BEAST *turns away with a low moan. Already he anticipates missing her.*]

THE BEAST: Beast, send her to her father. Your Beauty will remain there and you will die of grief.

BEAUTY: No, Beast, I will never be the cause of your death. Seven days and I promise you I will return.

THE BEAST: Seven days without my Beauty?

> [*Pause.* THE BEAST *resolves himself. He takes off the ring which she will need to transport her there.*]

Go. I must bear it. Seven days? I will bear it. Farewell, Beauty.

> [*He leaves her the ring, then slowly departs. She watches him go with tenderness and thanks.*]

BEAUTY: A week. That is all, dear Beast.

> [*He is visible for a few seconds, then exits. She looks at the ring, then puts it on. The lights change. Music. The briefest of blackouts.*]

SCENE THREE

The sheep station, day. From the blackness comes strong barking. The lights fade up. BEAUTY *is gone.* PADDY *enters with a shovel, on guard.*

PADDY: Hush, Ballarat. Good dog. Now, who have yer surprised in Beauty's room? Whether it's spear or pistol that waits for me behind that door, Paddy'll give you a go.

> [BEAUTY *enters behind* PADDY. *He does not see her. Barks come from offstage.*]

Quiet, Ballarat. I've got him.

[*The barking stops and* PADDY *waits.* BEAUTY *stands behind him and slowly puts her hands over his eyes. He jumps.*]
What's this? Those aren't bushranger's hands. I know the shape of this ring. The ring the beast gave to ... Strike me handsome, is it little Beauty?

[*He turns. They embrace.*]

[*Shouting*] Ryan. Will yer come in here, mate! Oh, Beauty. Beauty! We'd all but given you away.

BEAUTY: Dear Paddy.

[*They embrace again.* RYAN *enters.*]

PADDY: Ryan, will yer look who's here, mate?

[RYAN'*s eyes widen. His hands go out. He faints.* PADDY *rushes to break his fall.*]

BEAUTY: Father. Dear Father.

[*They crowd around him.*]

PADDY: It's alright now, mate. [*To* BEAUTY] He's been mopey as a wet hen, Beauty. [*To* RYAN] Didn't I always tell yer she'd come back?

[RYAN *revives.* PADDY *leaves them to their reunion.*]

RYAN: Beauty. Me little Beauty.

BEAUTY: Oh, Father.

RYAN: Beauty. Beauty.

BEAUTY: Father, so thin and worn.

RYAN: What? Not any more. Oh, Beauty.

BEAUTY: Oh, Father.

[*They embrace.* PADDY *returns excitedly with the magic mirror.*]

PADDY: I don't believe me eyes. I'd swear on a bag of boomerangs there was nothin there a second ago. Outside the humpy this, and a trunk full of the most prettiest dresses that you wouldn't find in Sydney.

BEAUTY: Oh, Beast, such kindness, when all you are feeling is loss. Paddy, do something for me. Find the two finest dresses in that chest and give them to my sisters.

PADDY: Surely, Beauty, your beast means those dresses for your use.

BEAUTY: Paddy!

PADDY: So, draggin' the chain gets ya dresses now, does it? I'll do it.

[*She gives him a look. He goes.*]

RYAN: The beast has sent you home to us. The same beast that was promisin' murder?

BEAUTY: Oh, Father, it's hard to believe that there was ever a killing thought in him. He is loving in a way that I have only known in you.

RYAN: Well, well ...

BEAUTY: And I have promised him I will not leave him for long.

RYAN: Oh, Beauty ...

BEAUTY: I have promised, Father.

[RYAN *shakes his head silently, sad again.*]

RYAN: But you're alive. You're alive! And more beautiful than ever.

BEAUTY: I have been well cared for.

[*Offstage, the sisters squeal with delight.* BEAUTY *and* RYAN *watch what happens.*]

RYAN: Will yer look at the girls? A good thought, Beauty. Don't they look fine in their silver and their gold. Look, they run to thank you. Oh, no!

BEAUTY: What has happened?

RYAN: Oh, no! Paddy was right. Your beast meant them only for you. The dresses are disappearin' off them.

[BEAUTY *cannot help breaking out into giggles.* RYAN *follows. The sisters enter in their underclothes.*]

BERNADETTE: Dear Beauty, thank you for these beautiful ...

BRIDIE: Yes, tha- ... Sister, your dress is vanished.

BERNADETTE: And so is yours!

BOTH: Ahhh.

[*They cover themselves, embarrassed.*]

BERNADETTE: Paddy, turn your back.

[BEAUTY *and* RYAN *laugh.*]

BOTH: [*to* BEAUTY] Ohhh!

RYAN: Girls! The beast intended these dresses only for Beauty. And could Beauty know? No harm done.

BERNADETTE: Thank you, Beauty. I hope we have provided some amusement on your return.

[*They turn their backs and sweep towards the exit.*]

BEAUTY: But sisters ...

[*They leave.* RYAN *and* BEAUTY *are still amused.*]

PADDY: Now then, I am going to put some tucker on the fire.
Tucker that will melt your heart.
RYAN: What tucker, Paddy? He's a blacksmith, Beauty, and
a water burner!
PADDY: I am not!
RYAN: What tucker, then?
PADDY: You may talk of the dishes of Paris renown.

                    ON MONDAY WE'VE MUTTON
[Singing]
                    Or for plenty through London may range.
                    If variety's pleasing, oh leave either town
                    And come to the bush for a change.
RYAN: Oh, no, no. Mercy. No! Not that again.
PADDY: Yes. *[Singing]*
                    On Monday we've mutton, with damper and
                        tea,
                    On Tuesday, tea damper and mutton.
                    Such dishes I'm certain all men must agree
                    Are fit for peer, peasant or glutton.

BEAUTY: ⎫
PADDY: ⎭ *[together, singing]*
                    On Wednesday we've damper with mutton and
                        tea,
                    On Thursday, tea, mutton and damper,
                    On Friday we've mutton tea damper, while we
                    With our flocks over hill and dale scamper.

RYAN: Paddy! Beauty is back. Something else. I beg ya!
PADDY: What's today, Ryan?
RYAN: Saturday.
PADDY: Then there is something else. Oh, Ryan, a banquet.
RYAN: What?
PADDY: *[singing]*
                    Our Saturday feast may seem rather strange -
RYAN: *[interrupting]* Nooo.
BEAUTY: ⎫
PADDY: ⎭ *[together, singing]*

'Tis of damper and tea and fine mutton.
Now surely I've shown you that plenty of
   change
In the bush is the friendly board put on.

RYAN: Enough. Enough. I'll starve. Beauty, how long can
you stay?

BEAUTY: Seven days, Father.

RYAN: Only seven?

BEAUTY: I promised.

PADDY: Seven is more than six.

   [*Pause.*]

RYAN: Seven is more than six.

   [*With the arms of both men around* BEAUTY, *they exit
joyfully. Fade down.*]

SCENE FOUR

Lights fade up on an empty clothes line. BRIDIE *and*
BERNADETTE *enter, each with a white sheet. As* BERNADETTE
speaks, they place the sheets over the line.

BERNADETTE: We work. She rests. [*Aping her father*] 'Oh,
my little Beauty.' [*Aping* BEAUTY] 'Oh, Father.' Sister,
how long have you said that someone would come for us?
To make us happy? Admit it that they will never come.
That we will scorch here under this cruel sun while she
lives happy with her beast.

   [*They finish placing the sheets.* BRIDIE *shields her eyes
from the sun.*]

BRIDIE: No. I will not endure her happiness. It mocks what I
suffer here.

BERNADETTE: Well, tomorrow we are rid of her.

   [*Pause.*]

BRIDIE: I wish our sister could stay longer.

BERNADETTE: What?

BRIDIE: Would her beast still be kind if Beauty did not return
on the seventh day?

BERNADETTE: Sister, come out of the sun.

BRIDIE: If our happy sister were late ... very late ... would not this animal turn fierce and angry?

BERNADETTE: Hmmm ...

BRIDIE: And on whom would he pour his jealousy?

BERNADETTE: On happy little Beauty.

BRIDIE: Hmmm ...

BERNADETTE: But we could not delay her. Even for a day. You see how anxious she has grown as the seventh day comes nearer.

BRIDIE: A single day is not enough. The animal would endure that. But three days, four days ...

BERNADETTE: But to delay her is impossible, sister.

    [BRIDIE *tests the sheet that is near her. It is already dry. She looks at the whiteness of the sheet.*]

BRIDIE: No. Not impossible.

    [*To the astonishment of her sister,* BRIDIE *sweeps the sheet from the line and twirls it around herself.*]

Sister, how will we look in white?

BERNADETTE: What?

    [BRIDIE *hums the first bar of 'The Wedding March'.* BERNADETTE *laughs.*]

Yes. Yes.

    [BERNADETTE *grabs the other sheet and twirls it around herself. They go off loudly humming 'The Wedding March', very pleased with themselves. Fade to blackout briefly as the music echoes the 'March'.*]

SCENE FIVE

The house of THE BEAST. *He enters slowly and painfully, holding the rose.*

THE BEAST: Seven days. Seven years. Without Beauty. Her laughter. Her company. Her voice. Her!

THE DYING STOCKMAN'S LAMENT

[*Singing*]
> 'Wrap me up in my stockwhip and blanket
> And bury me deep down below,
> Where the dingoes and crows cannot find me
> In the shade where the coolabahs grow.'

[*The lights start to fade.*]
Oh, come back, Beauty. Come back.
[*Fade to blackout.*]

SCENE SIX

The sheep station, day. Music. The lights come up as RYAN
and PADDY *enter.*

PADDY: No, mate!
RYAN: A day longer.
PADDY: This is already the eighth.
RYAN: Paddy ...
PADDY: No! Do not ask her.
RYAN: She must eat first.
PADDY: No. Will you have her break a promise? Listen, mate, you made a promise too and it didn't turn out too bad.
RYAN: I lost me daughter through it, Paddy.
PADDY: What? And her gettin' on like a bushfire with her beast?
RYAN: What will I do without her, Paddy?
PADDY: She's comin'. Crack hardy. Say nothin' that'll upset her more than she is already.
   [BEAUTY *enters, ready to leave.*]
BEAUTY: Oh, Father. Please smile.
   [PADDY *kicks him and he dredges up a smile.*]
RYAN: I am stronger now, Beauty, for yer visit. And will you ask him if he'll let yer return?
BEAUTY: I will, Father. And knowing him as I have come to do, I am sure he will say 'Yes'. Paddy.

PADDY: Don't you worry about us old reefers. Knowing you are happy, Beauty, then we will be happy. Won't we, Ryan? [*No response.* PADDY *kicks him.*]
I said, 'Won't we, Ryan?'

RYAN: We will.
[*He and* BEAUTY *embrace.* BEAUTY *takes out the ring.*]

BEAUTY: Put the ring on me, Father, with your blessing.
[*She hands him the ring.* RYAN *smiles and takes her hand to slip the ring on.* BRIDIE *and* BERNADETTE *enter, giggling and excited.*]

BRIDIE: Oh, Beauty!

BERNADETTE: Beauty.

BEAUTY: Dear sisters.

BRIDIE: Before you go we wanted to share with you our most happy news.

BERNADETTE: We do.
[*They giggle.*]

RYAN: News? What news, girls?

BRIDIE: Father, you remember those two fine young fellas ...

BERNADETTE: The squatter's sons.

BRIDIE: From Ninginbilli? Who called on us last year?

BERNADETTE: Offering to help with the shearing?

PADDY: Fine young fellas, is it? And didn't youse send the both the them cockatoos packin', callin' them 'ugly, sunburnt ruffians'?

BERNADETTE: Oh, Paddy!

BRIDIE: Unwillingly at first, we now see in a new light, Beauty, the happiness you have found with the Beast.

BERNADETTE: Yes. And we have reconsidered, Father.

RYAN: Reconsidered?

BERNADETTE: The offers those handsome boys made us.

BEAUTY: What offers, Sister? No!

BRIDIE: Yes.
[*They both put out their hands to show rings.*]
With Father's permission we wish to be as happy as our sister and marry immediately.

BEAUTY: Oh, sisters.

BRIDIE: At home with your beast, remember us on our wedding day.

BERNADETTE: Oh, do. Now we will wave you goodbye.

[*They giggle again and hug each other.* RYAN *looks at* BEAUTY. *She looks at him.*]

PADDY: Ryan!

RYAN: I said nothin'.

PADDY: And don't.

[*Pause.* BEAUTY *is confused.*]

BEAUTY: Bernadette, Bridie, you say you wish to marry immediately.

BRIDIE: Oh, yes, as soon as the necessary arrangements have-

BEAUTY: [*interrupting*] Tomorrow?

BERNADETTE: I think the day after tomorrow.

BRIDIE: Or the day after that.

BERNADETTE: At the very latest the day after that. But please, Beauty, don't delay on our account.

[*They giggle again and whisper.* RYAN *looks at* BEAUTY.]

BEAUTY: I ...

RYAN: Beauty ...

PADDY: Ryan, will yer let her make up her own mind?

BRIDIE: Beauty, we are thankful enough that your happiness has brought some sense into our hearts. Go.

[RYAN *pleads wordlessly with* BEAUTY *to stay for the family event.*]

BEAUTY: Oh, Father. I am sure that the dear Beast ... A few days. Sisters, let me share in your wedding day.

RYAN: Oh, Beauty.

BEAUTY: Three days?

BERNADETTE: Four ...

BRIDIE: At the very most. Four.

[BEAUTY *is worried but makes up her mind. She runs to her sisters and embraces them.*]

PADDY: Then into the humpy. Mustn't we toast the brides to be?

[RYAN *embraces* BEAUTY *thankfully. Exeunt. Fade to blackout.*]

SCENE SEVEN

The house of THE BEAST. *The music changes and the lights fade up as* THE BEAST *enters, close to death.*

THE BEAST: Beauty, you have left me and how can I blame you? I do not blame you. Such ugliness, such beauty. Beauty and the Beast. Now, like all stricken animals, I will not lie down to die in the glaring sun. I will find some shade, some darkness and there breathe my last. Oh, Beauty, but your Beast loved you.
[THE BEAST *groans as he slowly and painfully departs.*]

SCENE EIGHT

The sheep station, day. BEAUTY *enters, distraught, looking into her mirror.*

BEAUTY: I see an empty house. I see an empty garden. Beast, where are you? Be strong. The wedding day is here at last. I will soon be with you.
[BRIDIE *and* BERNADETTE *enter in ordinary country clothes.*]
Bernadette! Bridie! It is sixteen miles to the church. And you are not dressed for your wedding. Please hurry. I must be gone.
BERNADETTE: Wedding?
BRIDIE: What wedding?
[*Pause.* BEAUTY'*s hands go up in horror.*]
BEAUTY: Nooo!
BRIDIE: You think we are going to marry sunburnt cockatoos? We are meant for better. No. You marry. Marry your beast.
[*They laugh.*]
BEAUTY: Why? Why?
BRIDIE: Our lives have shrivelled in the sun while you laughed with your beast. See if he still laughs, Beauty.
BEAUTY: Out of my way! Beast, be strong! Wait for me!

[BEAUTY *exits. The girls congratulate themselves on their ruse. Suddenly something strikes* BRIDIE.]

BRIDIE: Our father!

BERNADETTE: If he finds out what we have done ...

BRIDIE: Cry, sister, and leave Father to me. Cry!

[BERNADETTE *starts to cry.* RYAN *ands* PADDY *enter animatedly.*]

RYAN: What's happenin'? Where is Beauty?

BERNADETTE: Gone to her beast.

PADDY: The weddin'?

BRIDIE: Oh, Father! The young men have changed their minds.

RYAN: What?

BRIDIE: And Father, only now do we realise that this delay for our dear sister may put her in great danger.

RYAN: What?

BRIDIE: Father, she has been with us for twelve days. You know what the Beast is like in his anger.

RYAN: No!

BRIDIE: He may kill our sister.

RYAN: No. No. No. Paddy?

PADDY: Yer know more than I, mate. Yer've seen him.

BRIDIE: Father, you know the place where you came upon his house.

RYAN: Paddy, get the guns. We will rescue her and bring her back to stay with us forever.

BRIDIE: Oh, Father, we hope so, we hope so.

[RYAN *and* PADDY *exit.*]

BERNADETTE: Sister!

BRIDIE: The Beast's house is full of riches. If we own it, then they will come. The richest men in the country. They will come then.

[*Exeunt. The lights fade briefly to blackout.*]

SCENE NINE

The house of THE BEAST. *The lights fade up on the rose in the vase.* BEAUTY *enters quickly, distraught.*

BEAUTY: Dear Beast, where are you? Why did it take so long for me to come to know that I love you? Beast, where are you? I love you.

>[*She reaches out to the rose. It's petals fall to the ground. She recalls his words, steps back and screams.*]

Nooo!

>[*She runs off. Enter* RYAN *and* PADDY, *searching.* PADDY *goes to the rose.*]

PADDY: Ryan! A dyin' rose. The one yer picked for Beauty so long ago.

RYAN: [*calling*] Beauty!

>[PADDY *picks up the petals.*]

PADDY: He kept the flower which brought Beauty to him, mate. Is our Beauty in danger from such a creature?

RYAN: Yes.

PADDY: This house has the smell of death, but it isn't Beauty's.

RYAN: He is a dangerous animal. Whose death, then?

PADDY: Our journey here, mate, set me thinkin'. These girls of yours. Them that would kid you up a tree and then chop it down. What did they ever care for but gold and silver? They've seen how Beauty has grown to care for this creature. They might kill him for that.

RYAN: What? No. Paddy! I know I've maybe spoilt them a little and they're wilful. But murder? No.

PADDY: Ryan, she's your favourite. They hate yer for that.

RYAN: Hate? Their own da?

PADDY: But most I reckon they hate her.

>[*Pause.* RYAN *moves off quickly.*]

RYAN: [*calling*] Beauty? Beauty?

>[PADDY *exits after him.* BERNADETTE *and* BRIDIE *enter with guns.*]

BERNADETTE: The rose. The Beast is close.

BRIDIE: Such treasures. Richer than she told us of. With the Beast and Beauty dead, we would live here.

BERNADETTE: No sweating cockatoos then, Sister.

BRIDIE: The richest men in the world. If we shoot straight.

[*Exeunt, guns at the ready, as the lights fade to blackout.*]

SCENE TEN

The garden of THE BEAST'*s house, day. There is a huddled shape on the ground.* BEAUTY *enters, distracted, and does not see it.*

BEAUTY: My Beast, you are here, somewhere in this dark and overgrown place. If you can hear me ... call out, dear Beast. However faint, I will hear you.

[*Pause. The huddled figure makes a feeble movement.*]

THE BEAST: [*feebly*] Beauty!

BEAUTY: My Beast. I've found you, my love. Oh, don't die. Don't die.

[*She bends over him.* BERNADETTE *and* BRIDIE *enter with guns.*]

BERNADETTE: Out of the way, Sister.

BRIDIE: That creature must die.

BEAUTY: Nooo.

[*She puts herself in front of the huddled figure. They shoot.*]

BEAUTY: Ahhh.

[BEAUTY *falls.*]

BRIDIE: Die for your beast if you must. It won't save him.

BERNADETTE: You think we will let these riches waste on an animal and a shearing girl?

[THE BEAST *groans and moves slightly.*]

He still lives. Quickly!

[*As they raise their guns,* RYAN *enters.*]

RYAN: Beauty!

BERNADETTE: ⎫
BRIDIE: ⎭ [*together*] Father!

RYAN: Girls, stop! Beauty.

BRIDIE: Stay back, Father. This was not meant for your eyes.

RYAN: Youse'd kill your own da?

BRIDIE: You have killed us, Father, with a life of poverty.

RYAN: Daughters!

BRIDIE: You must die, Father, so we may live.

> [*They raise their guns. From the audience comes a loud
> scream.*]

PADDY: Nooo.

> [*The girls swing their guns round. At this moment a figure
> rises from the skin of the dying* BEAST: a young man of
> imposing looks and demeanour.]

THE BEAST: Stop, both of you! Or you will suffer a worse fate
than being locked for years, as I have been, in the form of
a beast.

BRIDIE: Bernadette, shoot!

THE BEAST: Your guns have no power here. This house, this
garden are enchanted, as I have been by the spirits of this
land. Only to be released when a woman came to love this
animal for what is good in him and could forget the ugliness
of his form. This woman did so and now the curse of these
spirits leaves me and falls on you.

BRIDIE: You have no weapon. [*To* BERNADETTE] Shoot!

> [*They shoot, but to no effect.*]

THE BEAST: For all your wickedness, you will be rooted to this
spot and live like the trees here: frozen forever.

> [*They freeze.* RYAN *runs to the fallen* BEAUTY.]

RYAN: Beauty. Oh, my Beauty.

THE BEAST: Rise up, Beauty. You are not harmed. Nor could
be in this enchanted garden.

> [BEAUTY *starts to recover.*]

RYAN: Beauty.

BEAUTY: Where is my Beast?

THE BEAST: Here. Beauty, it is you who have saved me from
my prison in that skin. Now I can ask you, as myself, the
question I came to you so often in the evening to ask.

BEAUTY: I came back to the Beast today to change my answer.

[*They embrace.*]

Father. Paddy. The Beast. My husband.

RYAN: Beauty.

THE BEAST: You have nothing to fear from me. Your Beauty will live near you for as long as you live.

RYAN: Oh, Beauty.

THE BEAST: And Paddy. I have heard so much good of you that I am sure we will be friends.

[PADDY *and* THE BEAST *embrace.* RYAN *and* BEAUTY *embrace.*]

BEAUTY: Beauty and her Beast.

THE END

Also from Currency

To Chris, Geoff and Malcolm

and especially to my Mum.

Tim Aris as the Beast in *Beauty and the Beast*. Magpie Theatre production. Photo: Eric Algra.